*First Print Edition [1.0] -1438 h. (2017 c.e.)*

Copyright © 1438 H./2017 C.E.
**Taalib al-Ilm Educational Resources**

**http://taalib.com**
**Learn Islaam, Live Islaam.**ᔆᴹ

*ISBN EAN-13:*          978-1-938117-7-50-3     [Soft cover Print Edition]

## From the Publisher

## Golden Words Upon Golden Words...For Every Muslim.

"Imaam al-Barbahaaree, may Allaah have mercy upon him said:

**May Allaah have mercy upon you! Examine carefully the speech of everyone you hear from in your time particularly. So do not act in haste and do not enter into anything from it until you ask and see: Did any of the Companions of the Prophet, may Allaah's praise and salutations be upon him, speak about it, or did any of the scholars? So if you find a narration from them about it, cling to it, do not go beyond it for anything and do not give precedence to anything over it and thus fall into the Fire.**

Explanation by Sheikh Saaleh al-Fauzaan, may Allaah preserve him:

'Do not be hasty in accepting as correct what you may hear from the people, especially in these later times. As now there are many who speak about so many various matters, issuing rulings and ascribing to themselves both knowledge and the right to speak. This is especially the case after the emergence and spread of new modern day media technologies. Such that everyone now can speak and bring forth that which is, in truth, worthless; by this, meaning words of no true value - speaking about whatever they wish in the name of knowledge and in the name of the religion of Islaam. It has even reached the point that you find the people of misguidance and the members of the various groups of misguidance and deviance from the religion speaking as well. Such individuals have now become those who speak in the name of the religion of Islaam through means such as the various satellite television channels. Therefore be very cautious!

It is upon you, oh Muslim, and upon you, oh student of knowledge, individually, to verify matters and not rush to embrace everything and anything you may hear. It is upon you to verify the truth of what you hear, asking, 'Who else also makes this same statement or claim?', 'Where did this thought or concept originate or come from?', 'Who is its reference or source authority?' Asking what are the evidences which support it from within the Book and the Sunnah? And inquiring where has the individual who is putting this forth studied and taken his knowledge from? From who has he studied the knowledge of Islaam?

Each of these matters requires verification through inquiry and investigation, especially in the present age and time. It is not every speaker who should rightly be considered a source of knowledge, even if he is well spoken and eloquent and can manipulate words captivating his listeners. Do not be taken in and accept him until you are aware of the degree and scope of what he possesses of knowledge and understanding. Perhaps someone's words may be few, but possess true understanding, and perhaps another will have a great deal of speech yet he is actually ignorant to such a degree that he doesn't actually possess anything of true understanding. Rather he only has the ability to enchant with his speech so that the people are deceived. Yet he puts forth the perception that he is a scholar, that he is someone of true understanding and comprehension, that he is a capable thinker, and so forth. Through such means and ways he is able to deceive and beguile the people, taking them away from the way of truth.

Therefore, what is to be given true consideration is not the amount of the speech put forth or that one can extensively discuss a subject. Rather, the criterion that is to be given consideration is what that speech contains within it of sound authentic knowledge, what it contains of the established and transmitted principles of Islaam. Perhaps a short or brief statement which is connected to or has a foundation in the established principles can be of greater benefit than a great deal of speech which simply rambles on, and through hearing you don't actually receive very much benefit from.

This is the reality which is present in our time; one sees a tremendous amount of speech which only possesses within it a small amount of actual knowledge. We see the presence of many speakers, yet few people of true understanding and comprehension.' "

*[The eminent major scholar Sheikh Saaleh al-Fauzaan, may Allaah preserve him- 'A Valued Gift for the Reader Of Comments Upon the Book Sharh as-Sunnah', page 102-103]*

❦ *Is not He better than your so-called gods, He Who originates creation and shall then repeat it, and Who provides for you from heaven and earth? Is there any god with Allaah? Say: 'Bring forth your proofs, if you are truthful.'* ❧ -(Surah an-Naml: 64)

*Explanation:* ❦ ***Say: "Bring forth your proofs..*** ❧ This is a command for the Prophet, may Allaah's praise and salutation be upon him, to rebuke them immediately after they had put forward their own rebuke. Meaning: '*Say to them: bring your proof, whether it is an intellectual proof or a proof from transmitted knowledge, that would stand as evidence that there is another with Allaah, the Most Glorified and the Most Exalted*'. Additionally, it has been said that it means: '*Bring your proof that there is anyone other than Allaah, the Most High, who is capable of doing that which has been mentioned from His actions, the Most Glorified and the Most Exalted.*' ❦ ***...if you are truthful.*** ❧ meaning, in this claim. From this it is derived that a claim is not accepted unless clearly indicated by evidences."

[Tafseer al-'Aloosee: vol. 15, page 14]

Sheikh Rabee'a Ibn Hadee Umair al-Madkhalee, may Allaah preserve him said,

'It is possible for someone to simply say, "*So and so said such and such.*" However we should say, "*Produce your proof.*" So why did you not ask them for their proof by saying to them: "*Where was this said?*" Ask them questions such as this, as from your weapons are such questions as: "*Where is this from? From which book? From which cassette?...*" '

[The Overwhelming Falsehoods of 'Abdul-Lateef Bashmeel' page 14]

The guiding scholar Imaam Sheikh 'Abdul-'Azeez Ibn Abdullah Ibn Baaz, may Allaah have mercy upon him, said,

'It is not proper that any intelligent individual be misled or deceived by the great numbers from among people from the various countries who engage in such a practice. As the truth is not determined by the numerous people who engage in a matter, rather the truth is known by the Sharee'ah evidences. Just as Allaah the Most High says in Surah al-Baqarah, ❦ ***And they say, "None shall enter Paradise unless he be a Jew or a Christian." These are only their own desires. Say "Produce your proof if you are truthful."*** ❧ -(Surah al-Baqarah: 111) And Allaah the Most High says ❦ ***And if you obey most of those on the earth, they will mislead you far away from Allaah's path. They follow nothing but conjectures, and they do nothing but lie.*** ❧ -(Surah al-'Ana'an: 116)'

[Collection of Rulings and Various Statements of Sheikh Ibn Baaz -Vol. 1 page 85]

Sheikh Muhammad Ibn 'Abdul-Wahaab, may Allaah have mercy upon him, said,

'Additionally, verify that knowledge held regarding your beliefs, distinguishing between what is correct and false within it, coming to understand the various areas of knowledge of faith in Allaah alone and the required disbelief in all other objects of worship. You will certainly see various different matters which are called towards and enjoined; so if you see that a matter is in fact one coming from Allaah and His Messenger, then this is what is intended and is desired that you possess. Otherwise, Allaah has certainly given you that which enables you to distinguish between truth and falsehood, if Allaah so wills.

Moreover, this writing of mine- do not conceal it from the author of that work; rather present it to him. He may repent and affirm its truthfulness and then return to the guidance of Allaah, or perhaps if he says that he has a proof for his claims, even if that is only a single statement, or if he claims that within my statements there is something unsupported, then request his evidence for that assertion. After this if there is something which continues to cause uncertainty or is a problem for you, then refer it back to me, so that then you are aware of both his statement and mine in that issue. We ask Allaah to guide us, you, and all the Muslims to that which He loves and is pleased with.'

*[Personal Letters of Sheikh Muhammad Ibn 'Abdul-Wahaab- Conclusion to Letter 20]*

Sheikh 'Abdullah Ibn 'Abdur-Rahman Abu Bateen, may Allaah have mercy upon him, said,

'And for an individual, if it becomes clear to him that something is the truth, he should not turn away from it and or be discouraged simply due to the few people who agree with him and the many who oppose him in that, especially in these latter days of this present age.

If the ignorant one says: "*If this was the truth so and so and so and so would have been aware of it!*" However this is the very claim of the disbelievers, in their statement found in the Qur'aan ❨ *If it had truly been good, they would not have preceded us to it!*❩-(Surah al-Ahqaaf: 11) and in their statement ❨ *Is it these whom Allaah has favored from amongst us?*❩-(Surah al-Ana'am: 53). Yet certainly, as Alee Ibn Abee Taalib, may Allaah be pleased with him, stated "*Know the truth and then you will know it' people.*" But for the one who generally stands upon confusion and uncertainty, then every doubt swirls around him. And if the majority of the people were in fact upon the truth today, then Islaam would not be considered strange, yet, by Allaah, it is today seen as the most strange of affairs!"

*[Durar As-Sanneeyyah -vol. 10, page 400]*

An Educational Course Based Upon:

# Beneficial Answers to Questions On Innovated Methodologies

By the Guiding Scholar

*Sheikh Saaleh Ibn Fauzaan al-Fauzaan*

(may Allaah preserve him)

*Twenty Lessons on The Knowledge, Beliefs, & Methodology of Islaam*

[Exercise Workbook]

Compiled and Translated by:

Abu Sukhailah Khalil Ibn-Abelahyi

[1] METHODOLOGY & SECTS

## How to use this Exercise Workbook

This workbook can be used to make it simpler for the one administering a study circle to check all lesson homework, quizzes and exams from the answer key which is available at the back of the [Self Study / Teachers Edition]. The exercise workbooks can be collected after class or at another convenient time for student work to be checked before proceeding to the next lesson.

A small marking area has been added for indicating correct and incorrect answers at the bottom of each page. Depending on question type , there is a [ /1] or [ / 3 ]for recording the number of correct answers out of total answers on that specific page. Partial scores can be given for essay answers that may not completely fulfill the needed answer, and then clarifying notes added at the teacher notes section below the same essay answer area. In addition, there is there is also an final total correct area i.e. =[ /50] at the end of each section for recording the total number of correct answers for each individual lesson, quiz, or the final exam.

### SCORING EACH LESSON ASSESSMENT TOTAL

Multiply the total points of correct answers (max. 15) times (X) 6.7 for score out of 100.

### SCORING EACH QUIZ ASSESSMENT TOTAL

Multiply the total points of correct answers (max. 20) times (X) 5 for score out of 100.

### SCORING EACH FINAL EXAM ASSESSMENT TOTAL

Multiply the total points of correct answers (max. 50) times (X) 2 for score out of 100.

Sheikh 'Abdul-Muhsin al-'Abaad, may Allaah preserve him, was asked:

*Question: "We now hear many of the students of knowledge saying: '(We hear) so and so is not upon the correct methodology, such and such group is not upon the correct methodology, or so and so has left or gone out of the correct methodology'. But we don't know what is really intended by this term, methodology?! Rather this is a newly invented phrase! ...So I hold the position that it is not correct to use this word."*

The Sheikh responded: "Every individual has a methodology and every individual has a way and a path, and his path is that affair which he connects and commits himself to. So the general methodology of the People of the Sunnah and the Jama'ah in their beliefs and actions is: adherence to the Book of Allaah and the Sunnah, and giving precedence to the source texts. It restricts reliance upon the intellects and depends fully upon transmitted knowledge. As for others from those groups and sects which oppose the People of the Sunnah and the Jama'ah, then they rely firstly upon their intellects and then restrictively turn to transmitted knowledge. Therefore the clear meaning of methodology is: a path and way proceeded upon. Furthermore, the general methodology of the People of the Sunnah and the Jama'ah in their beliefs is: The acceptance and following of transmitted knowledge and full reliance upon that...

...As such if it is said "The methodology of such and such group is..." Then the meaning of this is: The path and way that they rely upon is such and such in relation to beliefs, and such and such in relation to actions, and such and such in regarding to interacting with the people. This is the methodology that they have put in place for themselves, and a path that they have brought forth and developed for themselves. And, as I previously stated, those who do this, bring forth a different methodology, are the people of innovation in the religion..."

*[From the transcribed explanation of Sunan Abu Dawood by the esteemed sheikh page 287]*

# TABLE OF CONTENTS

## TEST YOUR UNDERSTANDING:

### TRUE & FALSE QUESTIONS

*[Circle the correct letter for each individual sentence from today's content.]*

**3** min

01. As long as the book is good and from a reliable scholar, the   [T / F]
    beginner can benefit from any book in his studies.

02. The correct way to gain knowledge of Islaam is to give priority   [T / F]
    to taking knowledge directly from the scholars.

03. There is a lot of confusion among Muslims today about who   [T / F]
    are actually those scholars to guide the affairs of the Muslims.

### FILL IN THE BLANK QUESTIONS

*[Enter the correct individual words to complete the sentences from today's content.]*

**6** min

04. The Muslim beginning to study his religion regularly should start by
    selecting _____ books along with the _____ of
    trustworthy scholars for those works.

05. The good places for learning _____ knowledge are reliable schools
    and _____ faculties which teach students in _____ stages.
    After this we should study with the scholars in the _____.

06. Muslims who learn poorly in the incorrect way may fall into _____
    claiming knowledge, issuing incorrect _____, and speaking about
    Allaah _____ _____.

## COMPREHENSIVE UNDERSTANDING QUESTIONS

07.   Give one possible example of the harm causes by Muslims wrongly or falsely taking some individuals as knowledgable scholars. Explain some of the harms that came from that.

7-12 min

TEACHER NOTES / CORRECTIONS

*[  / 3 ]

7-12min

08. Give an example of a reliable book of knowledge studied with an explanation coming from a reliable scholar.

TEACHER NOTES / CORRECTIONS

09. Discuss two reasons in our modern age why people wrongly take people as scholars, when they are not, and how someone could avoid both.

_____
_____
_____
_____
_____
_____
_____
_____
_____
_____
_____
_____
_____
_____
_____
_____
_____
_____
_____
_____
_____
_____
_____

TEACHER NOTES / CORRECTIONS

_____
_____
_____
_____
_____

*[ / 3]=[ / 15]

## TEST YOUR UNDERSTANDING:

### TRUE & FALSE QUESTIONS

*[Circle the correct letter for each individual sentence from today's content.]*

01.  The scholars whom we choose to take knowledge from should [T / F] have certain beneficial qualities and characteristics.

02.  We can generally take knowledge from anyone who offers it to [T / F] us.

03.  Surah al-Fatihah describes those people who we should take [T / F] knowledge from and those we should not.

### FILL IN THE BLANK QUESTIONS

*[Enter the correct individual words to complete the sentences from today's content.]*

04.  It is _____ permissible to take knowledge from _____, even if they may be scholars.

05.  The people who are being blessed and have gained Allaah's favor are those who combine beneficial _____ and righteous _____.

06.  True scholars combine between the qualities of _____ knowledge, _____ beliefs, and _____ deeds..

## COMPREHENSIVE UNDERSTANDING QUESTIONS

07. Where is Sharee'ah knowledge described and found, and what significant benefit can we obtain from it?

7-12 min

_____

TEACHER NOTES / CORRECTIONS

*[ / 3 ]

08.    Give three specific examples of what is considered Sharee'ah knowledge.

TEACHER NOTES / CORRECTIONS

09. Describe two things that some Muslims give more importance to than first gaining Sharee'ah knowledge. For each one explain a possible harm that comes from this.

_____

_____

_____

_____

_____

_____

_____

_____

_____

_____

_____

_____

_____

_____

_____

_____

_____

_____

_____

_____

_____

_____

TEACHER NOTES / CORRECTIONS

_____

_____

_____

_____

_____

*[ /3]=[ /15]

LESSON - 03

## TEST YOUR UNDERSTANDING:

### TRUE & FALSE QUESTIONS

*[Circle the correct letter for each individual sentence from today's content.]*

3min

01. Every individual has a general way, or methodology, in their [T / F] life.

02. Methodology means having the correct beliefs about Allaah. [T / F]

03. Different methodologies are connected to different people and [T / F] their inward beliefs and outward practices.

### FILL IN THE BLANK QUESTIONS

*[Enter the correct individual words to complete the sentences from today's content.]*

04. If someone is upon the methodology of _____ and the methodology of the _____ _____, he will be from the inhabitants of Paradise.

6min

05. A person's methodology is his path in that affair which he _____ and _____ himself to.

06. Methodology is that general path which an individual walks upon in practicing both the _____ of the religion and its _____ matters.

## COMPREHENSIVE UNDERSTANDING QUESTIONS

7-12 min

LESSON - 03

07. List one misguided methodology among Muslims falsely connected to Islaam, plus one other misguided methodology from disbelievers outside of the bounds of Islaam. Then list one prominent personality known to proceed upon each of these two separate methodologies.

TEACHER NOTES / CORRECTIONS

*[  / 3 ]

08. Briefly explain one possible reason why some Muslims do not want there to be discussions about the methodology of Islaam?

_____

_____

_____

_____

_____

_____

_____

_____

_____

_____

_____

_____

_____

_____

_____

_____

_____

_____

_____

_____

_____

_____

_____

TEACHER NOTES / CORRECTIONS

_____

_____

_____

_____

_____

_____

[ / 3 ]✳

09. List any two separate misguided groups or movements among the Muslims and briefly explain one way each of their invented methodologies differs from that of the first generations of believers.

_____

_____

_____

_____

_____

_____

_____

_____

_____

_____

_____

_____

_____

_____

_____

_____

_____

_____

_____

_____

_____

_____

_____

| TEACHER NOTES / CORRECTIONS |
| --- |

_____

_____

_____

_____

_____

✻[ / 3]=[ / 15]

**TEST YOUR UNDERSTANDING:**

LESSON - 04

## TRUE & FALSE QUESTIONS

*[Circle the correct letter for each individual sentence from today's content.]*

01. A Muslim's aqeedah, or beliefs, is not connected to their minhaj    [T / F]
    or methodology.

02. A Muslims general way, or minhaj, includes many different    [T / F]
    areas of life.

03. The Companions took their fundamental beliefs from the    [T / F]
    Prophet but developed their own separate way of calling to
    Allaah and establishing Islaam among the Muslims.

**3**min

## FILL IN THE BLANK QUESTIONS

*[Enter the correct individual words to complete the sentences from today's content.]*

04. The word or term minhaj (methodology) is _____ in meaning
    than the term 'aqeedah or _____.

05. A Muslim's methodology or general path follows and comes from their
    essential _____ and its foundation is their inward _____.

06. The _____ of a Muslim and his _____ are in fact
    a single connected matter.

**6**min

## COMPREHENSIVE UNDERSTANDING QUESTIONS

**7-12** min

07. Give an example of any authentic belief in Islaam and how it is reflected in what we do in our daily lives.

TEACHER NOTES / CORRECTIONS

✳[ / 3 ]

**7-12**min

08. Give an example of a group who has established a new methodology or way of calling and establishing Islaam, and give one general reason why their developed methodology is incorrect.

_____

_____

_____

_____

_____

_____

_____

_____

_____

_____

_____

_____

_____

_____

_____

_____

_____

_____

_____

_____

_____

_____

_____

_____

_____

| TEACHER NOTES / CORRECTIONS |
| --- |

_____

_____

_____

_____

_____

09. List one belief of the heart, one statement of the tongue, and one deed of the limbs that reflect the correct methodology of Islaam.

TEACHER NOTES / CORRECTIONS

*[ / 3]=[ / 15]

**LESSON - 05**

3 min

6 min

## TEST YOUR UNDERSTANDING:

### TRUE & FALSE QUESTIONS

*[Circle the correct letter for each individual sentence from today's content.]*

01. The scholars of Islaam have never used descriptive terms for those who were adhering to the correct way of Islaam. [T / F]

02. Descriptive names from the scholars reflect the realities of people's understanding and practice. [T / F]

03. No one claims to follow Islaam except those who actually follow the way of the first Muslims. [T / F]

### FILL IN THE BLANK QUESTIONS

*[Enter the correct individual words to complete the sentences from today's content.]*

04. The Jamaa'ah are those Muslims standing steadfast upon the _____ when the other sects deviated due to their _____ and chose _____.

05. The people of the Sunnah are those who are _____ from or haven't been affected by _____.

06. One meaning of the word Sunnah is the _____ of _____.

## COMPREHENSIVE UNDERSTANDING QUESTIONS

**7-12**min

07. Describe two mentioned descriptive names of the guided Muslims, and explain why that specific name is valid.

TEACHER NOTES / CORRECTIONS

✱[ / 3 ]

08. Describe two mentioned descriptive names of the misguided or astray Muslims, and explain why that specific name is valid.

TEACHER NOTES / CORRECTIONS

09. Discuss one specific negative outcome for Muslims if the people fail to take time to distinguish and identify who is actually following the evidenced beliefs and practices of Islaam.

7-12 min

TEACHER NOTES / CORRECTIONS

✳[ / 3]=[ / 15]

## TEST YOUR UNDERSTANDING:

LESSON - 06

### TRUE & FALSE QUESTIONS

*[Circle the correct letter for each individual sentence from today's content.]*

01. There is no guarantee that there will always be Muslims upon   [T / F]
the true guidance of the last Prophet and Messenger.

02. This Ummah is protected from ever completely leaving aspects   [T / F]
of the guidance they were given in understanding and practice.

03. The foundation of Islaam will always be what the Prophet and   [T / F]
his Companions believed and practiced.

### FILL IN THE BLANK QUESTIONS

*[Enter the correct individual words to complete the sentences from today's content.]*

04. The Muslim Ummah will _____ up into _____-
_____ sects.

05. Allaah warns those who knowingly contradict and _____ the
Messenger after the _____ path has been _____ clearly
to him, with Hellfire.

06. Allaah said He is _____with the Muhaajireen and the Ansaar,
and also those who _____ them _____ (in Faith).

## COMPREHENSIVE UNDERSTANDING QUESTIONS

**7-12**min

07. Give two specific characteristics which distinguish the saved sect from misguided Muslims

---
---
---
---
---
---
---
---
---
---
---
---
---
---
---
---
---
---
---
---
---
---

| TEACHER NOTES / CORRECTIONS |
| --- |

---
---
---
---
---

*[ / 3 ]

08. Give a possible reason why some Muslims from the misguided sects would oppose and have hatred for the specific scholars of the Sunnah.

TEACHER NOTES / CORRECTIONS

09. List two well-known scholars in our modern age whom, if a person loves them, it is a sign of their connection to the Sunnah. Describe something those scholars did which led the Muslims upon the Sunnah to love them.

LESSON - 06

TEACHER NOTES / CORRECTIONS

*[ / 3]=[ / 15]

## TEST YOUR UNDERSTANDING:

### TRUE & FALSE QUESTIONS

*[Circle the correct letter for each individual sentence from today's content.]*

01. Historically and specifically, the Salaf were the Companions [T / F]
(Sahaabah), the Successors (Taabi'een), and the third righteous
generation after them.

02. The Prophet did not advise us to hold on to anything other [T / F]
than the Qur'aan and Sunnah.

03. When misguided groups increased among Muslims, the people [T / F]
of truth openly professed their ascription to the Salaf.

### FILL IN THE BLANK QUESTIONS

*[Enter the correct individual words to complete the sentences from today's content.]*

04. The Companions of Allaah's Messenger, had the most _____
hearts, the most profound _____ of Islaam.

05. The madhhab, or way of the _____, the first _____
generations, is nothing but the _____.

06. Ibn Mas'ood advised the Muslims to follow those righteous who have
_____, since a _____ person is never safe from
_____.

## COMPREHENSIVE UNDERSTANDING QUESTIONS

7-12 min

07. Give an example of any mentioned group or sect and one general way that they differ from the methodology of the Salaf.

TEACHER NOTES / CORRECTIONS

*[ / 3]

08. Give one example of how those who attribute or connect themselves to the first generations are not like modern day groups or movements among the Muslims.

_____

_____

_____

_____

_____

_____

_____

_____

_____

_____

_____

_____

_____

_____

_____

_____

_____

_____

_____

_____

_____

_____

_____

TEACHER NOTES / CORRECTIONS

_____

_____

_____

_____

_____

_____

09. The term Salafeeyah refers to the people of guidance. Give another example of a praiseworthy description that refers to one of the sources they adhere to, and explain what it means.

TEACHER NOTES / CORRECTIONS

## QUIZ 1- LEVEL 1: TEST YOUR UNDERSTANDING:

### TRUE & FALSE QUESTIONS [1 point each]
*[Circle the correct letter for each individual sentence for this section.]*

**7-12**min

QUIZ 1 -ONE

01. True Islamic education among Muslims spreads gradually and slowly. [T / F]

02. We take Sharee'ah knowledge from proficient scholars upon any methodology, new or old. [T / F]

03. Every individual has a methodology of how they understand and practice Islaam. [T / F]

04. Our aqeedah, or beliefs, includes every issue related to the unseen world Allaah created. [T / F]

05. The people of the Sunnah are those who are free from accepting innovations in the religion. [T / F]

06. There will always be some Muslims somewhere in the world practicing Islaam correctly, inwardly and outwardly. [T / F]

07. Allaah did not specifically praise the first Muslims nor those who followed them in the Qur'aan. [T / F]

## FILL IN THE BLANK QUESTIONS [1 point each]

*[Enter the correct individual words to complete the sentences for this section.]*

08.     The correct way to gain Sharee'ah knowledge is to seek it from the _____ upon the _____ of the first _____ of Muslims.

09.   It is not _____ to take from those who have deviations in their _____ related to shirk or negation of Allaah's _____.

10.   The true _____ reflect their _____. It is not simply theory or words memorized with no _____,

11.   Methodology includes the _____ of all the _____ of the religion, as well as its _____.

12,   Generally one's methodology _____ and comes from their essential _____,

13.   The 'Jamaa'ah' is the body of _____ standing always _____ upon the truth, whereas the other _____ are those who deviate from the _____.

14.   The two _____ terms used by the Prophet, the _____ group and the _____ sect, both refer to those Muslims who _____ upon his guidance.

## COMPREHENSIVE UNDERSTANDING QUESTIONS

**7-12** min

15. Give two examples of ways in which you personally gained Sharee'ah knowledge. List a third way that you haven't, but would like to use in the future.

TEACHER NOTES / CORRECTIONS

16. Describe of one of the descriptive names for the Muslims who remained upon the Prophet's guidance and give an example that reflects that characteristic.

TEACHER NOTES / CORRECTIONS

[ Multiply the total points of correct answers for all sections (max. 20) times (X5) for score out of 100.]

*[ / 3]=[ / 20]

## TEST YOUR UNDERSTANDING:

### TRUE & FALSE QUESTIONS
*[Circle the correct letter for each individual sentence from today's content.]*

01. The Muslim Brotherhood group strives to gather together all [T / F] of the different kinds of Muslims, including innovators and people of desires.

02. The group Jama'at at-Tableegh does not hold that the most [T / F] important foundation for Muslims to understand is the details of properly worshiping Allaah alone.

03. Calling Muslims to only understand Islaam as the Companions [T / F] understood it only causes problems.

### FILL IN THE BLANK QUESTIONS
*[Enter the correct individual words to complete the sentences from today's content.]*

04. The one who calls to _____ and the way of the _____, calls to true _____.

05. When divided and following various _____, the Muslims will _____ be able to stand before their _____.

06. It is not _____ for a person to simply submit and accept the _____ of _____.

LESSON - 08

3 min

6 min

### COMPREHENSIVE UNDERSTANDING QUESTIONS

**7-12**min

07.   Why is it important for a Muslim to read and be aware of the real differences between those who strive to adhere to the Sunnah and those who affiliate themselves with the sect of the Shee'ah?

_____

_____

_____

_____

_____

_____

_____

LESSON - 08

_____

_____

_____

_____

_____

_____

_____

_____

_____

_____

_____

| TEACHER NOTES / CORRECTIONS |
| --- |

_____

_____

_____

_____

✳[ / 3 ]

08. What is an important difference in how we take from the statements of the Messenger of Allaah, and how we take statements from anyone other than him? Briefly explain why that is the case.

_____

_____

_____

_____

_____

_____

_____

_____

_____

LESSON - 08

_____

_____

_____

_____

_____

_____

_____

_____

_____

_____

_____

_____

_____

_____

_____

TEACHER NOTES / CORRECTIONS

_____

_____

_____

_____

_____

[ / 3 ]*

09. How does the acceptance of the false principle, "We will implement together what we agree on and overlook one another in what we disagree on," affect the dealings of Muslims without firm Sharee'ah knowledge?

TEACHER NOTES / CORRECTIONS

*[ /3]=[ /15]

## TEST YOUR UNDERSTANDING:

### TRUE & FALSE QUESTIONS

*[Circle the correct letter for each individual sentence from today's content.]*

01. The Sharee'ah of Allaah is generally implemented in the [T / F] kingdom of Saudi Arabia.

02. Saudi Arabia as a whole, has always had various different [T / F] methodologies of Islaam in the modern age.

03. Many benefits and forms of good occur from the young [T / F] Muslims connecting them to the scholars upon the Sunnah.

### FILL IN THE BLANK QUESTIONS

*[Enter the correct individual words to complete the sentences from today's content.]*

04. Scholars advise the youth to not easily _____ every _____ offering them knowledge, when the youth do not _____ their beliefs or _____.

05. It is _____ to know both the _____ of knowledge of someone, and _____ he took knowledge from, when considering _____ with an individual.

06. Allaah has made the _____ the _____ of the Prophet Muhammad generally, for every _____ and _____ of the earth after him.

3 min

6 min

LESSON - 09

## COMPREHENSIVE UNDERSTANDING QUESTIONS

7-12 min

07. Discuss one of the main roles or functions that the guided senior scholars serve within the Muslim Ummah, and why some groups want to distance people from the scholars generally?

LESSON - 09

TEACHER NOTES / CORRECTIONS

*[ /3]

08. Why can't it be assumed that everyone who was a teacher or professor at one of the universities in Saudi Arabia is upon the Sunnah, when it is generally a land that follows the Sunnah?

TEACHER NOTES / CORRECTIONS

09. Is it correct to generally restrict taking knowledge from only specific upright scholars when there are also other upright people of knowledge? Give one example, whether modern time or from the past, to show your answer.

TEACHER NOTES / CORRECTIONS

## TEST YOUR UNDERSTANDING:

### TRUE & FALSE QUESTIONS

*[Circle the correct letter for each individual sentence from today's content.]*

01. Every matter that would bring the Muslim Ummah closer to   [T / F]
    Allaah was explained to us by the Messenger of Allaah.

02. We should affiliate with everyone who says they follow the   [T / F]
    Sunnah, regardless of whether their beliefs and deeds actually
    reflect this or not.

03. The seventy-two sects, not fully upon what the Messenger and   [T / F]
    his Companions were upon, stand under the threat of receiving
    Allaah's punishment in Hellfire.

LESSON - 10

### FILL IN THE BLANK QUESTIONS

*[Enter the correct individual words to complete the sentences from today's content.]*

04. The Muslims through time, upon the _____ of the Messenger
    and his _____, are the Jamaa'ah which we _____
    ourselves to and _____ with.

05. When looking at "Islamic" groups, _____ is not given to
    _____, it is only given to the_____ and_____.

06. Calling to _____ and His revealed religion is from the
    _____ of means of gaining_____ to Allaah, whereas
    calling to some _____, party, or movement is misguidance

## COMPREHENSIVE UNDERSTANDING QUESTIONS

7-12 min

07. Give three specific examples of matters which the Muslims differ about today even though they all say they follow the religion of Islaam.

LESSON - 10

TEACHER NOTES / CORRECTIONS

*[ / 3 ]

08. Give a example of one command the Messenger of Allaah gave to us regarding differing, and one warning he gave us in regarding it.

TEACHER NOTES / CORRECTIONS

09. Name one misguided sect from previous centuries and indicate one matter that distinguishes it, and name one misguided group or movement from our modern age and indicate one matter that distinguishes it.

TEACHER NOTES / CORRECTIONS

*[ / 3]=[ / 15]

## TEST YOUR UNDERSTANDING:

### TRUE & FALSE QUESTIONS

*[Circle the correct letter for each individual sentence from today's content.]*

01.  Criticizing the people involved in innovation in the religion   [T / F]
separates and weakens the Ummah.

02.  Islaam affirms the principle, 'The ends justifies the means,' or   [T / F]
'By any means necessary.'

03.  Islaam united the first Muslims as brothers upon a single set   [T / F]
of beliefs and methodology, practiced inwardly and outwardly.

### FILL IN THE BLANK QUESTIONS

*[Enter the correct individual words to complete the sentences from today's content.]*

04.  Those whom Allaah has bestowed His _____ on are those
who hold a correct _____ and a correct _____.

05.  Nothing unites the _____ and unifies the ranks except for
the statement of _____, when its meaning is _____
and its requirements are _____ upon.

06.  Those who try to _____ the people in spite of their different
specific _____ and varying _____ will inevitably
_____.

## COMPREHENSIVE UNDERSTANDING QUESTIONS

7-12 min

07. Give examples of two incorrect "means" or methods that some Muslims use to try and establish Islaam. Briefly explain why each is incorrect according to the guidance of Islaam.

_____

_____

_____

_____

_____

_____

_____

_____

_____

_____

_____

_____

_____

LESSON - 11

_____

_____

_____

_____

_____

_____

_____

_____

_____

| TEACHER NOTES / CORRECTIONS |
| --- |

_____

_____

_____

_____

*[ / 3 ]

7-12 min

08. Give a possible example of how when Muslims are united upon a single sets of beliefs and methodology they are protected from having true differing among themselves.

TEACHER NOTES / CORRECTIONS

09. Give an example of a misguided group, sect, or movement that utilizes secrecy as a fundamental way to spread their ideas, principles, and efforts.

7-12 min

LESSON - 11

TEACHER NOTES / CORRECTIONS

*[ / 3]=[ / 15]

## TEST YOUR UNDERSTANDING:

### TRUE & FALSE QUESTIONS

*[Circle the correct letter for each individual sentence from today's content.]*

01. There is no problem with befriending and socializing with [T / F] members of groups upon misguidance, without calling them to the truth and without explaining that to them.

02. The Companions did not strive to call those with innovations [T / F] back to the Sunnah, they just cooperated with them in what they agreed upon, and excused their errors.

03. Allaah does not consider guided the person who does not [T / F] consider those first Muslims guided.

### FILL IN THE BLANK QUESTIONS

*[Enter the correct individual words to complete the sentences from today's content.]*

**LESSON - 12**

04. It is permissible for some Muslims with firm _____ and insight to interact with other Muslims who have _____ in order to call them to _____ their errors and _____ onto the Sunnah.

05. In determining what is good or beneficial, _____ should only be given to what the _____ supports, not simply what the _____ act upon.

06. Every statement connected to the principles of _____ which does not find its _____ in the _____ period of Islaam, may be _____ and turned away from.

## COMPREHENSIVE UNDERSTANDING QUESTIONS

**7-12**min

07.    Give an example of a trial or practical problem someone may encounter because of a weakness in knowledge they have.

LESSON - 12

TEACHER NOTES / CORRECTIONS

*[ /3 ]

08. What is the goal intended when some of the knowledgable Muslims interact with other Muslims upon misguidance? Why is this not something that every Muslim can undertake?

TEACHER NOTES / CORRECTIONS

09. Give the example of a false belief or practice that a group or sect holds as true, which was completely unknown to any of the Companions.

7-12 min

_____

_____

_____

_____

_____

_____

_____

_____

_____

_____

_____

_____

_____

_____

_____

_____

_____

_____

LESSON - 12

_____

_____

_____

_____

_____

_____

| TEACHER NOTES / CORRECTIONS |
| --- |

_____

_____

_____

_____

_____

*[ /3]=[ /15]

## TEST YOUR UNDERSTANDING:

### TRUE & FALSE QUESTIONS

*[Circle the correct letter for each individual sentence from today's content.]*

01. Some groups among the Muslims have some fundamental opposition [T / F] to the Book of Allaah and the Sunnah.

02. Those Muslims who say that the terrorist explosions in the land of [T / F] the disbelievers are just, lack any support at all for this in the revealed source texts, and only follow their desires.

03. There are clear characteristics that distinguish someone who has [T / F] affiliated himself towards a group or organization, separate from Jamaa'ah of Muslims.

### FILL IN THE BLANK QUESTIONS

*[Enter the correct individual words to complete the sentences from today's content.]*

04. It is not correct to place or take any _____, other than the Prophet, from among the _____ as someone whom we make our _____ and enmity based on him _____.

05. The people of _____ commonly place an individual leader and his personal _____ as the _____ source for themselves, above the _____ texts.

06. The followers of different _____ and movements _____ their leaders in the _____ they issue, without returning back to the Qur'aan and the Sunnah, or asking them for _____.

## COMPREHENSIVE UNDERSTANDING QUESTIONS

7-12 min

07. Give and briefly explain a possible example of how someone who has affiliated themselves with a group upon innovation will approach their religion differently because of that.

LESSON - 13

TEACHER NOTES / CORRECTIONS

✳[ / 3 ]

08. What would the people affiliated with innovated sects and groups gain by Muslims not discussing the matters in which they oppose the beliefs and methodology of the Prophet?

TEACHER NOTES / CORRECTIONS

09. Give three possible practical examples of how a young Muslim affiliated with a group of innovation today might interact with them digitally or online.

TEACHER NOTES / CORRECTIONS

*[ /3]=[ /15]

## QUIZ 2- LEVEL 1: TEST YOUR UNDERSTANDING:

### TRUE & FALSE QUESTIONS [1 point each]

*[Circle the correct letter for each individual sentence for this section.]*

**7-12**min

01. Calling to tawheed and the way of the Salaf brings unity and unifies the ranks, even if some dislike it. [T / F]

02. There are always guided scholars upon the Sunnah in every century and age. [T / F]

03. There are some ways to get to Jannah that the Prophet, may the praise and salutations of Allaah be upon him, did not inform and teach the Muslims about. [T / F]

04. Allaah will only unite the hearts of the believers upon tawheed and Muslims following way of the Companions and those who followed them. [T / F]

05. We do not have any general way of Islaam other than that which the Companions of the Messenger of Allaah stood upon. [T / F]

06. Ibn 'Abbaas, may Allaah be pleased with him, went to the Khawaarij and debated with them, refuting their misconceptions. [T / F]

07. It is a characteristic of those involved with partisan groups and organizations among the Muslims to criticize and speak against the legitimate Muslim rulers. [T / F]

QUIZ 2 -TWO

## FILL IN THE BLANK QUESTIONS [1 point each]

*[Enter the correct individual words to complete the sentences for this section.]*

08.    The Shee'ah _____ the people of the _____ and the _____ in every area of their religion.

09.    The country of _____ _____ has played a _____ role in this age in spreading of authentic _____.

10.    The true _____ is what has been gathered upon the path of the _____, may Allaah's praise and salutations be upon him, and his _____.

11.    The person who claims that _____ the people involved _____ in the religion, _____ the Ummah, is considered astray.

12,    The _____ among the seventy-three _____ of the Ummah is of the _____ type caused by opposing the _____.

13.    Ibn Mas'ood, may Allaah be pleased with him, went to those _____ who were in the _____, stopped by them and _____ their innovation.

14.    Terrorist _____ are not from the practices of _____ which have any evidence from the _____, and are totally prohibited.

## COMPREHENSIVE UNDERSTANDING QUESTIONS

15. Why do various innovated groups dislike the call to weigh and compare the details of the beliefs and practices of every sect or group against the Book of Allaah and the Sunnah?

QUIZ 2 -TWO

7-12 min

TEACHER NOTES / CORRECTIONS

16. Give an example of a leader of misguidance from a modern group, sect, or movement upon innovation, and one example of a false principle which that leader called to and spread among the Muslims.

TEACHER NOTES / CORRECTIONS

[ Multiply the total points of correct answers for all sections (max. 20) times (X5) for score out of 100.]

*[ / 3]=[ / 20]

## TEST YOUR UNDERSTANDING:

### TRUE & FALSE QUESTIONS

*[Circle the correct letter for each individual sentence from today's content.]*

01. Allaah places scholars in every time and age who defend, clarify, [T / F] and manifest the way of the Salaf.

02. Salafeeyah is a methodology coming from a specific individual [T / F] who came after the Messenger of Allaah.

03. Whenever needed, the scholars are patient when trying to [T / F] correct the mistakes someone has fallen into, hoping they return to what is correct.

### FILL IN THE BLANK QUESTIONS

*[Enter the correct individual words to complete the sentences from today's content.]*

04. Young Muslims should keep _____ from the _____ and the members of these _____ methodologies as well as their _____.

05. A_____ has an _____ on his student, and a _____ teacher can _____ a youth.

06. Salafeeyah, means _____ the methodology of the first _____ generations, in their beliefs, their statements, their _____, their cohesion, their unity, their _____, and their mutual_____ relations among themselves.

3 min

6 min

LESSON - 14

## COMPREHENSIVE UNDERSTANDING QUESTIONS

**7-12** min

07. Give an example of a possible negative effect that might occur among Muslims when those calling to the way of the Salaf do not fully reflect the true guidance of this way in one or more aspects.

LESSON - 14

TEACHER NOTES / CORRECTIONS

*[ / 3 ]

08. An important evidenced area of knowledge in Islaam is knowledge-based refutations. Name four other areas or branches of knowledge that are important in Islaam.

TEACHER NOTES / CORRECTIONS

09. Considering the example of Imaam Ahmad, briefly point out one way in which he refuted the people of innovation, and point out one way in which he strove in another branch of beneficial knowledge.

TEACHER NOTES / CORRECTIONS

*[ / 3]=[ / 15]

## TEST YOUR UNDERSTANDING:

### TRUE & FALSE QUESTIONS

*[Circle the correct letter for each individual sentence from today's content.]*

**3**min

01. There is no danger in responding to and listening to callers [T / F] upon what might be paths of misguidance because we are all Muslims.

02. The group Jamaa'at at-Tableegh invites to Islaam in a general [T / F] sense, but generally do not approve of efforts to teach the specific authentic beliefs about which Muslims disagree.

03. Allaah and His Messenger informed us that there would appear [T / F] sects in opposition to the unified body of Ahlus-Sunnah wal-Jamaa'ah.

### FILL IN THE BLANK QUESTIONS

*[Enter the correct individual words to complete the sentences from today's content.]*

**6**min

**LESSON - 15**

04. The Messenger _____ the lines he drew saying about the _____ line: {This is the path of _____}, and about the _____ lines to the right and left: {These are the 'other' paths. Upon _____ path there is a devil calling the people to it.}.

05. Muslims, _____ and old, are obligated to _____ all of the groups and sects that _____ the unified body of Ahlus-Sunnah wal-Jamaa'ah, and to _____ against those who call to these groups.

06. Muslims have been _____ us to _____ to the Prophet's Sunnah and the _____ of the rightly _____ Khaleefahs who came after him.

## COMPREHENSIVE UNDERSTANDING QUESTIONS

**7-12** min

07.   Give an example of one essential criterion by which we can use to tell that a group or sect is upon misguidance. Then give one practical example of a matter of misguidance which a sect or group differ in according to that criterion.

LESSON - 15

TEACHER NOTES / CORRECTIONS

✳[ /3 ]

08. Why are general efforts to call to beneficial knowledge considered fighting against misguidance? Give a practical example of how a general Muslim striving upon the Sunnah could help a someone affected by misguidance through such efforts.

TEACHER NOTES / CORRECTIONS

09. What is one of the errors of Jamaa'at at-Tableegh regarding what they focus upon regarding tawheed? In the example mentioned, give one possible reason why the members of Jamaa'at at-Tableegh opposed his speaking among them from authentic knowledge.

7-12 min

LESSON - 15

TEACHER NOTES / CORRECTIONS

*[ / 3]=[ / 15]

## TEST YOUR UNDERSTANDING:

### TRUE & FALSE QUESTIONS

*[Circle the correct letter for each individual sentence from today's content.]*

**3min**

01. One type of caller of evil is someone who mixes the truth with falsehood and conceals the truth, even though they know it. [T / F]

02. Those people who ignorantly try to call to the truth without having firm knowledge, are not considered callers to what is correct and sound. [T / F]

03. There is benefit in studying the correct creed but no benefit in knowing about beliefs that oppose it. [T / F]

### FILL IN THE BLANK QUESTIONS

*[Enter the correct individual words to complete the sentences from today's content.]*

**6min**

04. When _____ knowledge of the Sunnah, we should take from those _____ who are trustworthy in their _____ and _____.

05. The Christians _____ Allaah without clear _____, evidences, or _____ that Allaah _____ the prophet 'Esaa with.

06. The Muslim who is _____ of an astray group's or sect's actual _____, should be _____ with evidence that they are people who are ignorant of the original religion and so are upon _____.

LESSON - 16

## COMPREHENSIVE UNDERSTANDING QUESTIONS

7-12 min

07. Give an example of one of the actions the Muslims striving upon the Sunnah must take in relation to other Muslims who knowingly proceed upon innovation in Islaam. What is a possible benefit for other general Muslims from what you mentioned?

TEACHER NOTES / CORRECTIONS

LESSON - 16

*[ / 3]

08. What priority should the Muslim begin with and build their religion upon? What is an incorrect alternative priority that some misguided Muslims have focused upon instead?

TEACHER NOTES / CORRECTIONS

09. Should we just immediately stop interacting with another Muslim who is seen to have close relations with someone upon of innovation? What is one of the steps some of the scholars advised we take, and what is the benefit of that step?

_____

_____

_____

_____

_____

_____

_____

_____

_____

_____

_____

_____

_____

_____

_____

_____

_____

_____

_____

_____

_____

_____

_____

_____

_____

LESSON - 16

| TEACHER NOTES / CORRECTIONS |
| --- |

_____

_____

_____

_____

_____

_____

✳[ /3]=[ /15]

## TEST YOUR UNDERSTANDING:

### TRUE & FALSE QUESTIONS

*[Circle the correct letter for each individual sentence from today's content.]*

**3**min

01. There are different ways for a Muslim to fall into a misguided [T / F] belief or misunderstanding and not realize it.

02. We should always try to study even specialized areas of Sharee'ah [T / F] knowledge with the people of the Sunnah.

03. General people may be deceived by the lack of a clear position of a [T / F] student of knowledge taking some knowledge from an innovator.

### FILL IN THE BLANK QUESTIONS

*[Enter the correct individual words to complete the sentences from today's content.]*

**6**min

04. The people of the _____ give importance to knowledge, as well as _____, and struggling against every form of_____.

05. The people of the Sunnah do not _____ a Muslim is a _____, even if he is an _____ in the religion, except when the innovation he knowingly accepts reaches the level of _____ disbelief.

06. Any good or _____ found within the _____ of the innovators, is also undoubtedly also found in the _____ of the Muslims following first _____ of believers.

LESSON - 17

### COMPREHENSIVE UNDERSTANDING QUESTIONS

**7-12** min

07. Give one example of a sect or group upon innovation that is not generally considered major disbelief, and one example of a sect upon innovation that is considered major disbelief. List one innovation from each of these two types of groups or sect.

_____

_____

_____

_____

_____

_____

_____

_____

_____

_____

_____

_____

_____

_____

_____

_____

_____

_____

_____

_____

_____

LESSON - 17

| TEACHER NOTES / CORRECTIONS |
| --- |

_____

_____

_____

_____

✳[ / 3 ]

08.     Give a practical example of how a Muslim may have unknowingly taken on a false belief which negates Allaah's name and attributes. When is such a person considered a disbeliever?

_____

_____

_____

_____

_____

_____

_____

_____

_____

_____

_____

_____

_____

_____

_____

_____

_____

_____

_____

_____

_____

_____

_____

_____

LESSON - 17

## TEACHER NOTES / CORRECTIONS

_____

_____

_____

_____

_____

[  /3]*

09. Give three possible examples of false beliefs someone may wrongly take from their teacher from among the misguided sects or groups present among the Muslims today.

7-12 min

_____

_____

_____

_____

_____

_____

_____

_____

_____

_____

_____

_____

_____

_____

_____

_____

_____

_____

_____

_____

_____

_____

_____

| TEACHER NOTES / CORRECTIONS |
| --- |

_____

_____

_____

_____

_____

*[ /3]=[ /15]

## TEST YOUR UNDERSTANDING:

### TRUE & FALSE QUESTIONS

*[Circle the correct letter for each individual sentence from today's content.]*

01.  Ibn 'Abbaas warned some Muslims about giving precedence to [T / F] the position of any of the people of knowledge above proofs from the revealed source texts.

02.  We follow the Sunnah except when it conflicts with the scholars [T / F] of our madhhab or historical school of fiqh.

03.  Only Allaah is loved for Himself alone, others are loved for His [T / F] sake and our love for them is connected to our love for Him.

**3**min

### FILL IN THE BLANK QUESTIONS

*[Enter the correct individual words to complete the sentences from today's content.]*

04.  It is _____ to follow the _____ whoever it is with, and not to follow individuals that _____ the truth.

05.  One cause of trials is the giving _____ and authority to our _____ over the revealed Sharee'ah and giving precedence to _____ over the sound _____ shaped by guidance.

06.  When considering two _____ scholastic positions, that specific position which you should _____ is the one which the Sharee'ah _____ indicate is the _____ position.

**6**min

LESSON - 18

## COMPREHENSIVE UNDERSTANDING QUESTIONS

**7-12** min

07. Give examples of two other sources that some Muslims incorrectly give full precedence to over the authentic guidance of the revealed source texts.

TEACHER NOTES / CORRECTIONS

LESSON - 18

*[ /3]

08. Give an example of a fiqh issue in which the modern day scholars are known to differ in. What is one possible reason why they came to legitimately different conclusions?

_____

_____

_____

_____

_____

_____

_____

_____

_____

_____

_____

_____

_____

_____

_____

_____

_____

_____

_____

_____

_____

_____

TEACHER NOTES / CORRECTIONS

09.     Give an example of how a person might diminish the role of the scholars in what he does in his own life, and an example showing how in his life he might go beyond the proper bounds in relation to a specific scholar.

TEACHER NOTES / CORRECTIONS

*[  /3]=[  /15]

## TEST YOUR UNDERSTANDING:

### TRUE & FALSE QUESTIONS

*[Circle the correct letter for each individual sentence from today's content.]*

01. We can accept, entirely, everything an individual says if he ia a well known scholar.   [T / F]

02. Blind fanaticism to an individual is detested, condemned, and not permissible.   [T / F]

03. There is no one that is infallible or protected from errors except Allaah's Messenger and the scholars.   [T / F]

**3** min

### FILL IN THE BLANK QUESTIONS

*[Enter the correct individual words to complete the sentences from today's content.]*

04. If one scholar makes a _____ in an issue, then other scholars should _____ the truth with regard to this issue, based upon _____.

05. When a scholar _____ another scholar or one of the noble personalities who is upon the Sunnah, this does _____ mean that we have a _____ for him or we are _____ him.

06. Clarifying _____ someone has made _____ falls under offering sincere _____ to all of the _____.

**6** min

LESSON - 19

## COMPREHENSIVE UNDERSTANDING QUESTIONS

**7-12** min

07. Name one mistake that someone can make in reference to the statements of the scholars. List one misconception that may have led to that mistake.

_____

_____

_____

_____

_____

_____

_____

_____

_____

_____

_____

_____

_____

_____

_____

_____

_____

_____

_____

_____

_____

_____

_____

_____

TEACHER NOTES / CORRECTIONS

_____

_____

_____

_____

LESSON - 19

*[ /3 ]

08. List two mistakes that people fall into regarding the different independently derived positions in a specific matter that occur between scholars both upon the Sunnah.

_____

_____

_____

_____

_____

_____

_____

_____

_____

_____

_____

_____

_____

_____

_____

_____

_____

_____

_____

_____

_____

_____

_____

| TEACHER NOTES / CORRECTIONS |
| --- |

_____

_____

_____

_____

_____

[ /3]*

09. What is one of the most important mentioned reasons we follow and take from the scholars? And how can we know that reason applies to a specific scholar?

_____

_____

_____

_____

_____

_____

_____

_____

_____

_____

_____

_____

_____

_____

_____

_____

_____

_____

_____

_____

_____

_____

_____

_____

_____

_____

TEACHER NOTES / CORRECTIONS

_____

_____

LESSON - 19

_____

_____

_____

✳[ /3]=[ /15]

## TEST YOUR UNDERSTANDING:

### TRUE & FALSE QUESTIONS

*[Circle the correct letter for each individual sentence from today's content.]*

01. We will not be asked about what we did with the knowledge, [T / F] the prophets and messengers brought to humanity.

02. The methodology of the sect of Khawaarij and the sect of [T / F] Mu'tazilah toward Muslim rulers is correct.

03. The efforts upon way of the Salaf, of the first three generations, [T / F] has awakened the world of Islaam to again look at what is the correct Islaam in this century.

### FILL IN THE BLANK QUESTIONS

*[Enter the correct individual words to complete the sentences from today's content.]*

04. Our senior scholars _____ us to follow the methodology of the _____ and the _____ and the way of the predecessors of this Ummah when _____ and clarifying societal issues.

05. We can _____ our deeds, by placing and weighing them on the _____ of the Book of _____, the Sunnah, and the _____ of the pious predecessors of the Muslim Ummah.

06. A Muslim must _____ himself both from matters of associating _____ with Allaah, and free himself from the actual _____ that engage in directing their _____ to others than Allaah.

**3**min

**6**min

LESSON - 20

## COMPREHENSIVE UNDERSTANDING QUESTIONS

**7-12**min

07.   Describe two distinct characteristics of the call to understand and practice Islaam as the Salaf did.

_____

_____

_____

_____

_____

_____

_____

_____

_____

_____

_____

_____

_____

_____

_____

_____

_____

_____

_____

_____

_____

_____

| TEACHER NOTES / CORRECTIONS |
| --- |

_____

_____

_____

_____

LESSON - 20

*[ /3 ]

08. Describe one harmful effect upon the individual from those working to establish Islaam, but who have turned away from the methodology of the Salaf in doing so.

_____

_____

_____

_____

_____

_____

_____

_____

_____

_____

_____

_____

_____

_____

_____

_____

_____

_____

_____

_____

_____

_____

_____

_____

| TEACHER NOTES / CORRECTIONS |
| --- |

09. Describe one harmful effect upon Muslim societies from those working to establish Islaam, but who have turned away from the methodology of the Salaf in doing so.

-12 min

TEACHER NOTES / CORRECTIONS

97

LESSON - 20

*[ /3]=[ /15]

## FINAL- LEVEL 1: TEST YOUR UNDERSTANDING:

### TRUE & FALSE QUESTIONS [1 point each]

*[Circle the correct letter for each individual sentence for this section.]*

01. Today people have mixed individuals into the ranks of who are [T / F] considered Muslim scholars that do not belong there.

02. If a Muslim's methodology of understanding and practicing [T / F] Islaam through his life is correct, he will be from the inhabitants of Paradise.

03. Any scholar upon the Sunnah who has been criticized for a [T / F] mistake, it is impermissible to take knowledge from him.

04. We should join various Muslim groups just to work on those [T / F] things we agree upon with them, but not everything.

05. The praiseworthy descriptive terms and names of the Muslims [T / F] of guidance are not restricted to the Muslims of a specific time period, but can apply to all the guided Muslims.

06. What unites the hearts and unifies the ranks is our mutual [T / F] connection to Islaam, even if we differ in essential fundamental beliefs.

07. The Muslim countries are required by Islaam to fulfill all the [T / F] terms and conditions of the treaties they have agreed to with the disbelieving nations.

08. If a group or movement says that it is Islamic and working for [T / F] Islaam, then we should assume that it conforms to the guidance of the Qur'aan and authentic Sunnah.

09. Salafeeyah is a recent group from amongst the various groups [T / F] and parties among modern Muslims.

10. Not every innovator in Islaam has fallen into committing major [T / F] disbelief.

## FILL IN THE BLANK QUESTIONS [1 point each]

*[Enter the correct individual words to complete the sentences for this section.]*

11. The characteristics of a _____ learner of Sharee'ah knowledge are _____, patience, and _____.

12. The characteristics of those _____ whom we should take knowledge from are having _____ knowledge, sound _____, and righteous _____.

13. Aqeedah is every issue related to beliefs in the _____ world which is not connected to a specific _____ of an action or _____.

14. Absolute _____ following cannot be done towards anyone _____ the Messenger of Allaah, as he was made _____ and did not ever speak from his _____.

15. A distinguishing characteristic of Jamaa'at _____ is that they do not give the proper importance to calling to _____ nor to warning against _____.

16. The Muslim Brotherhood _____ are involved in calling people to _____ against the legitimate Muslim rulers, and overthrowing the governments through _____.

17. The misguided sects do not want for you to _____ Islaam upon its _____ reality as because this makes clear the _____ of what they presently _____ upon and claim.

18. The _____ of those who do not follow the Salaf are characterized by the _____ of the importance of focusing on the _____ of Allaah alone, and their practical acts of worship are tainted by _____ into the religion.

19. At times of _____ and splitting, the Prophet _____ us to stick to his Sunnah and the _____ of the rightly guided Khaleefahs, and to adhere to the _____ body of Muslims and _____ of the Muslims, if present.

20. It is incorrect to _____ and criticize those scholars who scholastically _____ and criticize others with _____, and label such scholars as those who are _____.

*[ / 10]

## COMPREHENSIVE UNDERSTANDING QUESTIONS

21. List three beneficial matters a student can take from someone who is a scholar.

_____

_____

_____

_____

_____

_____

_____

_____

_____

_____

_____

_____

_____

_____

_____

_____

_____

_____

_____

_____

_____

_____

_____

_____

_____

_____

_____

| TEACHER NOTES / CORRECTIONS |
| --- |

_____

_____

_____

_____

_____

22. Explain why it is important to consider and learn about the correct methodology of Islaam. What is one real danger in not learning about the methodology of Islaam which the Companions proceeded upon?

_____

_____

_____

_____

_____

_____

_____

_____

_____

_____

_____

_____

_____

_____

_____

_____

_____

_____

_____

_____

_____

_____

| TEACHER NOTES / CORRECTIONS |
|---|

_____

_____

_____

_____

FINAL EXAM

*[ / 3]

23. Give two examples of how methodology determines the main priority a Muslim has, one of correct priority from the people of the Sunnah, and one of incorrect or distorted priority from any of the misguided groups or movements.

_____

_____

_____

_____

_____

_____

_____

_____

_____

_____

_____

_____

_____

_____

_____

_____

_____

_____

_____

_____

_____

_____

| TEACHER NOTES / CORRECTIONS |
| --- |

24. What are two important characteristics of the true Jamaa'ah that remained upon the truth of original Islaam.

_____

_____

_____

_____

_____

_____

_____

_____

_____

_____

_____

_____

_____

_____

_____

_____

_____

_____

_____

_____

_____

_____

| TEACHER NOTES / CORRECTIONS |
| --- |

_____

_____

_____

_____

FINAL EXAM

*[ / 3]

25.   Discuss one essential characteristic of the guided Muslims which the Prophet himself informed us of. Why do the scholars hold that it is beneficial to use descriptive names for the people of guidance?

TEACHER NOTES / CORRECTIONS

26    Briefly describe any two distinguishing characteristics of the people who have fallen into the misguidance of group partisanship to a movement, group, or organization, present among the Muslim Ummah.

TEACHER NOTES / CORRECTIONS

*[ /3]

27. What is an acceptable reason some of the people of knowledge would mix with the people of innovation and misguidance. What is a condition for them to do so?

_____
_____
_____
_____
_____
_____
_____
_____
_____
_____
_____
_____
_____
_____
_____
_____
_____
_____
_____
_____
_____
_____
_____
_____

TEACHER NOTES / CORRECTIONS

_____
_____
_____
_____
_____

28. What is an incorrect unbalanced understanding of Salafeeyah that some scholars have mentioned? What is the correct balanced understanding that opposes this?

_____

_____

_____

_____

_____

_____

_____

_____

_____

_____

_____

_____

_____

_____

_____

_____

_____

_____

_____

_____

_____

| TEACHER NOTES / CORRECTIONS |
| --- |

_____

_____

_____

_____

FINAL EXAM

*[ /3]

29. What is the correct Sharee'ah position we should have towards our scholars? What are the extremes to this correct position.

_____
_____
_____
_____
_____
_____
_____
_____
_____
_____
_____
_____
_____
_____
_____
_____
_____
_____
_____
_____
_____

TEACHER NOTES / CORRECTIONS

_____
_____
_____

FINAL EXAM

30. Is one Salafee scholar discussing, clarifying, or refuting a mistake made by another Salafee scholar with evidences, attacking him, or is it acceptable? How do we know that scholars can be mistaken?

_____

_____

_____

_____

_____

_____

_____

_____

_____

_____

_____

_____

_____

_____

_____

_____

_____

_____

_____

_____

_____

_____

_____

| TEACHER NOTES / CORRECTIONS |
| --- |

_____

_____

_____

_____

**FINAL EXAM**

[ Multiply the total points of correct answers for all sections (max. 50) times (X2) for score out of 100.]

*109*

✳[    / 3]=[    / 50]

# THE NAKHLAH EDUCATIONAL SERIES:

The Purpose of the 'Nakhlah Educational Series' is to contribute to the present knowledge based efforts which enable Muslim individuals, families, and communities to understand and learn Islaam and then to develop withi,n and truly live, Islaam. Our commitment and goal is to contribute beneficial publications and works that:

Firstly, reflect the priority, message and methodology of all the prophets and messengers sent to humanity, meaning that single revealed message which embodies the very purpose of life, and of human creation. As Allaah the Most High has said,

❖ *We sent a Messenger to every nation ordering them that they should worship Allaah alone, obey Him and make their worship purely for Him, and that they should avoid everything worshipped besides Allaah. So from them there were those whom Allaah guided to His religion, and there were those who were unbelievers for whom misguidance was ordained. So travel through the land and see the destruction that befell those who denied the Messengers and disbelieved.*❖–(Surah an-Nahl: 36)

Sheikh Rabee'a ibn Haadee al-Madkhalee in his work entitled, '*The Methodology of the Prophets in Calling to Allaah, That is the Way of Wisdom and Intelligence.*' explains the essential, enduring message of all the prophets:

"*So what was the message which these noble, chosen men, may Allaah's praises and salutations of peace be upon them all, brought to their people? Indeed their mission encompassed every matter of good and distanced and restrained every matter of evil. They brought forth to mankind everything needed for their well-being and happiness in this world and the Hereafter. There is nothing good except that they guided the people towards it, and nothing evil except that they warned the people against it. ...*

*This was the message found with all of the Messengers; that they should guide to every good and warn against every evil. However where did they start, what did they begin with, and what did they concentrate upon? There are a number of essentials, basic principles, and fundamentals which all their calls were founded upon, and which were the starting point for calling the people to Allaah. These fundamental points and principles are: 1. The worship of Allaah alone without any associates 2. The sending of prophets to guide creation 3. The belief in the resurrection and the life of the Hereafter*

*These three principles are the area of commonality and unity within their calls, and stand as the fundamental principles which they were established upon. These principles are given the greatest importance in the Qur'aan and are fully explained in it. They are also its most important purpose upon which it centers and which it continually mentions. It further quotes intellectual and observable proofs for them in all its chapters as well as within most of its accounts of previous nations and given examples.*

*This is known to those who have full understanding, and are able to consider carefully and comprehend well. All the Books revealed by Allaah have given great importance to these points and all of the various revealed laws of guidance are agreed upon them. And the most important and sublime of these three principles, and the most fundamental of them all, is directing one's worship only towards Allaah alone, the Blessed and the Most High."*

Today one finds that there are indeed many paths, groups, and organizations apparently presenting themselves as representing Islaam, which struggle to put forth an outwardly pleasing appearance to the general Muslims; but when their methods are placed upon the precise scale of conforming to priorities and methodology of the message of the prophets sent by Allaah, they can only be recognized as deficient paths- not simply in practice but in principle- leading not to success, but rather only to inevitable failure.

As Sheikh Saaleh al-Fauzaan, may Allaah preserve him, states in his introduction to the same above-mentioned work on the methodology of all the prophets,

*"So whichever call is not built upon these foundations, and whatever methodology is not from the methodology of the Messengers - then it will be frustrated and fail, and it will be effort and toil without any benefit. The clearest proofs of this are those present-day groups and organizations which set out a methodology and program for themselves and their efforts of calling the people to Islaam which is different from the methodology of the Messengers. These groups have neglected the importance of the people having the correct belief and creed - except for a very few of them - and instead call for the correction of side-issues."*

There can be no true success in any form for us as individuals, families, or larger communities without making the encompassing worship of Allaah alone, with no partners or associates, the very and only foundation of our lives. It is necessary that each individual knowingly choose to base his life upon that same foundation taught by all the prophets and messengers sent by the Lord of all the worlds, rather than simply delving into the assorted secondary concerns and issues invited to by the various numerous parties, innovated movements, and groups. Indeed Sheikh al-Albaanee, may Allaah have mercy upon him, stated:

*"...We unreservedly combat against this way of having various different parties and groups. As this false way- of group or organizational allegiances - conforms to the statement of Allaah the Most High,* ◈ **But they have broken their religion among them into sects, each group rejoicing in what is with it as its beliefs. And every party is pleased with whatever they stand with.** ◈*—(Surah al-Mu'minoon: 53) And in truth they are no separate groups and parties in Islaam itself. There is only one true party, as is stated in a verse in the Qur'an,* ◈ **Verily, it is the party of Allaah that will be the successful.** ◈*—(Surah al-Mujadilaah: 58). The party of Allaah are those people who stand with the Messenger of Allaah, may Allaah's praise and salutations be upon him, meaning that an individual proceeds upon the methodology of the Companions of the Messenger. Due to this we call for having sound knowledge of the Book and the Sunnah."*

*(Knowledge Based Issues & Sharee'ah Rulings: The Rulings of The Guiding Scholar Sheikh Muhammad Naasiruddeen al-Albaanee Made in the City of Medina & In the Emirates – [Emiratee Fatwa no 114. P.30])*

## TWO ESSENTIAL FOUNDATIONS

Secondly, building upon the above foundation, our commitment is to contributing publications and works which reflect the inherited message and methodology of the acknowledged scholars of the many various branches of Sharee'ah knowledge, who stood upon the straight path of preserved guidance in every century and time since the time of our Messenger, may Allaah's praise and salutations be upon him. These people of knowledge, who are the inheritors of the Final Messenger, have always adhered closely to the two revealed sources of guidance: the Book of Allaah and the Sunnah of the Messenger of Allaah- may Allaah's praise and salutations be upon him, upon the united consensus, standing with the body of guided Muslims in every century - preserving and transmitting the true religion generation after generation. Indeed the Messenger of Allaah, may Allaah's praise and salutations be upon him, informed us that, *{ A group of people amongst my Ummah will remain obedient to Allaah's orders. They will not be harmed by those who leave them nor by those who oppose them, until Allaah's command for the Last Day comes upon them while they remain on the right path. }* (Authentically narrated in Saheeh al-Bukhaaree).

We live in an age in which the question frequently asked is, "*How do we make Islaam a reality?*" and perhaps the related and more fundamental question is, "*What is Islaam?*", such that innumerable different voices quickly stand to offer countless different conflicting answers through books, lectures, and every available form of modern media. Yet the only true course of properly understanding this question and its answer- for ourselves and our families -is to return to the criterion given to us by our beloved Messenger, may Allaah's praise and salutations be upon him. Indeed the Messenger of Allaah, may Allaah's praise and salutations be upon him, indicated in an authentic narration, clarifying the matter beyond doubt, that the only "Islaam" which enables one to be truly successful and saved in this world and the next is as he said, *{... that which I am upon and my Companions are upon today.}* (authentically narrated in Jaam'ea at-Tirmidhee) referring to that Islaam which stands upon unchanging revealed knowledge. While every other changed and altered form of Islaam, whether through some form of extremism or negligence, or through the addition or removal of something, regardless of whether that came from a good intention or an evil one- is not the religion that Allaah informed us about when He revealed, ◈ *This day, those who disbelieved have given up all hope of your religion; so fear them not, but fear Me. This day, I have perfected your religion for you, completed My Favor upon you, and have chosen for you Islaam as your religion.*◈–(Surah al-Maa'idah: 3)

The guiding scholar Sheikh al-Albaanee, may have mercy upon him, said,

"*...And specifically mentioning those among the callers who have taken upon themselves the guiding of the young Muslim generation upon Islaam, working to educate them with its education, and to socialize them with its culture. Yet they themselves have generally not attempted to unify their understanding of those matters about Islaam regarding which the people of Islaam today differ about so severely.*

And the situation is certainly not as is falsely supposed by some individuals from among them who are heedless or negligent - that the differences that exist among them are only in secondary matters without entering into or affecting the fundamental issues or principles of the religion; and the examples to prove that this is not true are numerous and recognized by those who have studied the books of the many differing groups and sects, or by the one who has knowledge of the various differing concepts and beliefs held by the Muslims today."(Mukhtasir al-'Uloo Lil'Alee al-Ghafaar, page 55)

Similarly he, may Allaah have mercy upon him, explained:

"Indeed, Islaam is the only solution, and this statement is something which the various different Islamic groups, organizations, and movements could never disagree about. And this is something which is from the blessings of Allaah upon the Muslims. However there are significant differences between the different Islamic groups, organizations, and movements that are present today regarding that domain which working within will bring about our rectification. What is that area of work to endeavor within, striving to restore a way of life truly reflecting Islaam, renewing that system of living which comes from Islaam, and in order to establish the Islamic government? The groups and movements significantly differ upon this issue or point. Yet we hold that it is required to begin with the matters of tasfeeyah –clarification, and tarbeeyah -education and cultivation, with both of them being undertaken together.

As if we were to start with the issue of governing and politics, then it has been seen that those who occupy themselves with this focus firstly possess beliefs which are clearly corrupted and ruined, and secondly that their personal behavior, from the aspect of conforming to Islaam, is very far from conforming to the actual guidance of the Sharee'ah. While those who first concern themselves with working just to unite the people and gather the masses together under a broad banner of the general term "Islaam," then it is seen that within the minds of those speakers who raise such calls -in reality there is in fact no actual clear understanding of what Islaam is. Moreover, the understanding they have of Islaam has no significant impact in starting to change and reform their own lives. Due to this reason, you find that many such individuals from here and there, who hold this perspective, are unable to truly realize or reflect Islaam, even in areas of their own personal lives in matters which it is in fact easily possible for them to implement. Such an individual holds that no one - regardless of whether it is because of his arrogance or pridefulness - can enter into directing him in an area of his personal life!

Yet at the same time these same individuals are raising their voices saying, "Judgment is only for Allaah!" and "It is required that judgment of affairs be according to what Allaah revealed." And this is indeed a true statement, but the one who does not possess something certainly cannot give or offer it to others. The majority of Muslims today have not established the judgment of Allaah fully upon themselves, yet they still seek from others to establish the judgment of Allaah within their governments...

*...And I understand that this issue or subject is not immune from there being those who oppose our methodology of tasfeeyah and tarbeeyah. As there is the one who would say, "But establishing this tasfeeyah and tarbeeyah is a matter which requires many long years!" So, I respond by saying, this is not an important consideration in this matter, what is important is that we carry out what we have been commanded to do within our religion and by our Mighty Lord. What is important is that we begin by properly understanding our religion first and foremost. After this is accomplished then it will not be important whether the road itself is long or short.*

*And indeed, I direct this statement of mine towards those men who are callers to the religion among the Muslims, and towards the scholars and those who direct our affairs. I call for them to stand upon complete knowledge of true Islaam, and to fight against every form of negligence and heedlessness regarding the religion, and against differing and disputes, as Allaah has said, ◈...**and do not dispute with one another for fear that you lose courage and your strength departs** ◈—(Surah al-Anfaal: 46). (Quoted from the work, 'The Life of Sheikh al-Albaanee, His Influence in Present Day Fields of Sharee'ah Knowledge, & the Praise of the Scholars for Him.' volume 1 page 380-385)*

The guiding scholar Sheikh Zayd al-Madkhalee, may Allaah protect him, stated in his writing, 'The Well Established Principles of the Way of the First Generations of Muslims: It's Enduring & Excellent Distinct Characteristics' that,

*"From among these principles and characteristics is that the methodology of tasfeeyah -or clarification, and tarbeeyah -or education and cultivation- is clearly affirmed and established as a true way coming from the first three generations of Islaam, and is something well known to the people of true merit from among them, as is concluded by considering all the related evidence. What is intended by tasfeeyah, when referring to it generally, is clarifying that which is the truth from that which is falsehood, what is goodness from that which is harmful and corrupt, and when referring to its specific meanings, it is distinguishing the noble Sunnah of the Prophet and the people of the Sunnah from those innovated matters brought into the religion and the people who are supporters of such innovations.*

*As for what is intended by tarbeeyah, it is calling all of the creation to take on the manners and embrace the excellent character invited to by that guidance revealed to them by their Lord through His worshiper and Messenger Muhammad, may Allaah's praise and salutations be upon him; so that they might have good character, manners, and behavior. As without this they cannot have a good life, nor can they put right their present condition or their final destination. And we seek refuge in Allaah from the evil of not being able to achieve that rectification."*

Thus the methodology of the people of standing upon the Prophet's Sunnah, and proceeding upon the 'way of the believers' in every century is reflected in a focus and concern with these two essential matters: tasfeeyah- or clarification of what is original, revealed message from the Lord of all the worlds, and tarbeeyah- or education and raising of ourselves, our families, and our communities, and our lands upon what has been distinguished to be that true message and path.

---

METHODOLOGY:

MISSION

The priority and focus of the 'Nakhlah Educational Series' is reflected within in the following statements of Sheikh al-Albaanee, may Allaah have mercy upon him:

*"As for the other obligation, then I intend by this the education of the young generation upon Islaam purified from all of those impurities we have mentioned, giving them a correct Islamic education from their very earliest years, without any influence of a foreign, disbelieving education."*

*(Silsilat al-Hadeeth ad-Da'eefah, Introduction page 2.)*

*"...And since the Messenger of Allaah, may Allaah's praise and salutations be upon him, has indicated that the only cure to remove this state of humiliation that we find ourselves entrenched within, is truly returning back to the religion, then it is clearly obligatory upon us - through the people of knowledge- to correctly and properly understand the religion in a way that conforms to the sources of the Book of Allaah and the Sunnah, and that we educate and raise a new virtuous, righteous generation upon this."*

*(Clarification and Cultivation and the Need of the Muslims for Them)*

It is essential, in discussing our perspective upon this obligation of raising the new generation of Muslims, that we highlight and bring attention to a required pillar of these efforts as indicated by Sheikh al-Albaanee, may Allaah have mercy upon him, and others- in the golden words, *"through the people of knowledge."* Something we commonly experience today is that many people have various incorrect understandings of the role that the scholars should have in the life of a Muslim, failing to understand the way in which they fulfill their position as the inheritors of the Messenger of Allaah, may Allaah's praise and salutations be upon him, and stand as those who preserve and enable us to practice the guidance of Islaam. Indeed, the noble Imaam Sheikh as-Sa'dee, may Allaah have mercy upon him, in his work, *"A Definitive and Clear Explanation of the Work 'A Triumph for the Saved Sect'"* pages 237-240, has explained this crucial issue with an extraordinary explanation full of remarkable benefits:

*"Section: Explaining the Conditions for These Two Source Texts to Suffice You -or the Finding of Sufficiency in these Two Sources of Revelation.*

*Overall the conditions needed to achieve this and bring it about return to two matters:*

*Firstly, the presence of the requirements necessary for achieving this; meaning a complete devotion to the Book and the Sunnah, and the putting forth of efforts both in seeking to understand their intended meanings, as well as in striving to be guided by them. What is required secondly is the pushing away of everything which prevents achieving this finding of sufficiency in them.*

This is through having a firm determination to distance yourself from everything which contradicts these two source texts in what comes from the historical schools of jurisprudence, assorted various statements, differing principles and their resulting conclusions which the majority of people proceed upon. These matters which contradict the two sources of revelation include many affairs which, when the worshiper of Allaah repels them from himself and stands against them, the realm of his knowledge, understanding, and deeds then expands greatly. Through a devotion to them and a complete dedication towards these two sources of revelation, proceeding upon every path which assists one's understanding them, and receiving enlightenment from the light of the scholars and being guided by the guidance that they possess- you will achieve that complete sufficiency in them. And surely, in the positions they take towards the leading people of knowledge and the scholars, the people are three types of individuals:

The first of them is the one who goes to extremes in his attachment to the scholars. He makes their statements something which are infallible as if their words held the same position as those of the statements of the Messenger of Allaah, may Allaah's praise and salutations be upon him, as well as giving those scholars' statements precedence and predominance over the Book of Allaah and the Sunnah. This is despite the fact that every leading scholar who has been accepted by this Ummah was one who promoted and encouraged the following of the Book and the Sunnah, commanding the people not to follow their own statements nor their school of thought in anything which stood in opposition to the Book of Allaah and the Sunnah.

The second type is the one who generally rejects and invalidates the statements of the scholars and forbids the referring to the statements of the leading scholars of guidance and those people of knowledge who stand as brilliant lamps in the darkness. This type of person neither relies upon the light of discernment with the scholars, nor utilizes their stores of knowledge. Or even if perhaps they do so, they do not direct thanks towards them for this. And this manner and way prohibits them from tremendous good. Furthermore, that which motivates such individuals to proceed in this way is their falsely supposing that the obligation to follow the Messenger of Allaah, may Allaah's praise and salutations be upon him, and the giving of precedence to his statements over the statements of anyone else, requires that they do so without any reliance upon the statements of the Companions, or those who followed them in goodness, or those leading scholars of guidance within the Ummah. This is a glaring and extraordinary mistake.

Indeed the Companions and the people of knowledge are the means and the agency between the Messenger of Allaah, may Allaah's praise and salutations be upon him, and his Ummah- in the transmission and spreading his Sunnah in regard to both its wording and texts, as well as its meanings and understanding. Therefore the one who follows them in what they convey in this is guided through their understandings, receives knowledge from the light they possess, benefits from the conclusions they have derived from these sources -of beneficial meanings and explanations, as well as in relation to subtle matters which scarcely occur to the minds of some of the other people of knowledge, or barely comes to be discerned by their minds. Consequently, from the blessing of Allaah upon this Ummah is that He has given them these guiding scholars who cultivate and educate them upon two clear types of excellent cultivation.

The first category is education from the direction of one's knowledge and understanding. They educate the Ummah upon the more essential and fundamental matters before the more complex affairs. They convey the meanings of the Book and the Sunnah to the minds and intellects of the people through efforts of teaching which rectifies, and through composing various beneficial books of knowledge which a worshiper doesn't even have the ability to adequately describe what is encompassed within them of aspects of knowledge and benefits. These works reflect the presence of a clear white hand in deriving guidance from the Book of Allaah and the Sunnah, and through the arrangement, detailed clarification, division and explanation, through the gathering together of explanations, comparisons, conditions, pillars, and explanations about that which prevents the fulfillment of matters, as well as distinguishing between differing meanings and categorizing various knowledge based benefits.

The second category is education from the direction of one's conduct and actions. They cultivate the peoples characters encouraging them towards every praiseworthy aspect of good character, through explaining its ruling and high status, and what benefits comes to be realized from it, clarifying the reasons and paths which enable one to attain it, as well as those affairs which prevent, delay, or hinder someone becoming one distinguished and characterized by it. Because they, in reality, are those who bring nourishment to the hearts and the souls; they are the doctors who treat the diseases of the heart and its defects. As such, they educate the people through their statements, and actions, as well as their general guided way. Therefore the scholars have a tremendous right over this Ummah. A portion of love and esteem, respect and honor, and thanks, are due to them because their merits and their various good efforts stand above every other right after establishing the right of Allaah, and the right of His Messenger, may Allaah's praise and salutations be upon him.

Because of this, the third group of individuals in respect to the scholars are those who have been guided to understand their true role and position, and establish their rights, thanking them for their virtues and merits, benefiting by taking from the knowledge they have, while acknowledging their rank and status. They understand that the scholars are not infallible and that their statements must stand in conformance to the statements of the Messenger of Allaah, may Allaah's praise and salutations be upon him, and that each one from among them has that which is from guidance, knowledge, and correctness in his statements taken and benefited from, while turning away from whatever in mistaken within it.

Yet such a scholar is not to be belittled for his mistake, as he stands as one who strove to reach the truth; therefore his mistake will be forgiven, and he should be thanked for his efforts. One clarifies what was stated by of any one of these leaders from among men, when it is recognized that it has some weakness or conflict to an evidence of the Sharee'ah, by explaining its weakness and the level of that weakness, without speaking evilly of the intention of those people of knowledge and religion, nor defaming them due to that error. Rather we say, as it is obligatory to say, "And those who came after them say: ❧ **Our Lord! forgive us and our brethren who have preceded us in faith, and put not in our hearts any hatred against those who have believed. Our Lord! You are indeed full of kindness, Most Merciful.** ❧ -(Surah al-Hashr: 10).

*Accordingly, individuals of this third type are those who fulfill two different matters. They join together on one hand between giving precedence to the Book and the Sunnah over everything else, and, on the other hand, between comprehending the level and position of the scholars and the leading people of knowledge and guidance, and establishing this even if it is only done in regard to some of their rights upon us. So we ask Allaah to bless us to be from this type, and to make us from among the people of this third type, and to make us from those who love Him and love those who love Him, and those who love every action which brings us closer to everything He loves."*

Upon this clarity regarding the proper understanding of our balanced position towards our guided Muslim scholars, consider the following words about the realm of work of the general people of faith, which explains our area of efforts and struggle as Muslim parents, found in the following statement by Sheikh Saaleh Fauzaan al-Fauzaan, may Allaah preserve him.

*"**Question: Some people mistakenly believe that calling to Allaah is a matter not to be undertaken by anyone else other than the scholars without exception, and that it is not something required for other than the scholars, according to that which they have knowledge of, to undertake any efforts of calling the people to Allaah. So what is your esteemed guidance regarding this?"***

The Sheikh responded by saying:

*"This is not a misconception, but is in fact a reality. The call to Allaah cannot be established except through those who are scholars, and I state this. Yet, certainly there are clear issues which every person understands. As such, every individual should enjoin the good and forbid wrongdoing according to the level of his understanding, such that he instructs and orders the members of his household to perform the ritual daily prayers and other matters that are clear and well known.*

*Undertaking this is something mandatory and required even upon the common people, such that they must command their children to perform their prayers in the masjid. The Messenger of Allaah, may Allaah praise and salutations be upon him, said, { **Command you children to pray at seven, and beat them due to its negligence at ten.**} (Authentic narration found in Sunan Abu Dawood ). And the Messenger of Allaah, may Allaah praise and salutations be upon him, said, { **Each one of you is a guardian or a shepherd, and each of you is responsible for those under his guardianship....**} (Authentic narration found in Saheeh al-Bukhaaree). So this is called guardianship, and this is also called enjoining the good and forbidding wrongdoing. The Messenger of Allaah, may Allaah praise and salutations be upon him, said, { **The one from among you who sees a wrong should change it with his hand, and if he is unable to do so, then with his tongue, and if he is not able to do this, then with his heart.** } (Authentic narration found in Saheeh Muslim).*

*So in relation to the common person, that which it is required from him to endeavor upon is that he commands the members of his household-as well as others -with the proper performance of the ritual prayers, the obligatory charity, with generally striving to obey Allaah, to stay away from sins and transgressions, that he purify and cleanse his home from disobedience, and that he educate and cultivate his children upon the obedience of Allaah's commands. This is what is required from him, even if he is a general person, as these types of matters are from that which is understood by every single person. This is something which is clear and apparent.*

MISSION

But as for the matters of putting forth rulings and judgments regarding matters in the religion, or entering into clarifying issues of what is permissible and what is forbidden, or explaining what is considered associating others in the worship due to Allaah and what is properly worshiping Him alone without any partner- then indeed these are matters which cannot be established except by the scholars"

(*Beneficial Responses to Questions About Modern Methodologies, Question 15, page 22*)

Similarly the guiding scholar Sheikh 'Abdul-'Azeez Ibn Baaz, may Allaah have mercy upon him, also emphasized this same overall responsibility:

"...*It is also upon a Muslim that he struggles diligently in that which will place his worldly affairs in a good state, just as he must also strive in the correcting of his religious affairs and the affairs of his own family. The people of his household have a significant right over him that he strive diligently in rectifying their affair and guiding them towards goodness, due to the statement of Allaah, the Most Exalted,* ◊ **Oh you who believe! Save yourselves and your families Hellfire whose fuel is men and stones** ◊ *-(Surah at-Tahreem: 6)*

*So it is upon you to strive to correct the affairs of the members of your family. This includes your wife, your children- both male and female- and such as your own brothers. This concerns all of the people in your family, meaning you should strive to teach them the religion, guiding and directing them, and warning them from those matters Allaah has prohibited for us. Because you are the one who is responsible for them as shown in the statement of the Prophet, may Allaah's praise and salutations be upon him,* { **Every one of you is a guardian, and responsible for what is in his custody. The ruler is a guardian of his subjects and responsible for them; a husband is a guardian of his family and is responsible for it; a lady is a guardian of her husband's house and is responsible for it, and a servant is a guardian of his master's property and is responsible for it....**} *Then the Messenger of Allaah, may Allaah's praise and salutations be upon him, continued to say,* {**...so all of you are guardians and are responsible for those under your authority.**} *(Authentically narrated in Saheeh al-Bukhaaree & Muslim)*

*It is upon us to strive diligently in correcting the affairs of the members of our families, from the aspect of purifying their sincerity of intention for Allaah's sake alone in all of their deeds, and ensuring that they truthfully believe in and follow the Messenger of Allaah, may Allaah's praise and salutations be upon him, their fulfilling the prayer and the other obligations which Allaah the Most Exalted has commanded for us, as well as from the direction of distancing them from everything which Allaah has prohibited.*

*It is upon every single man and woman to give advice to their families about the fulfillment of what is obligatory upon them. Certainly, it is upon the woman as well as upon the man to perform this. In this way our homes become corrected and rectified in regard to the most important and essential matters. Allaah said to His Prophet, may Allaah's praise and salutations be upon him,* ◊ **And enjoin the ritual prayers on your family...** ◊ *(Surah Taha: 132) Similarly, Allaah the Most Exalted said to His prophet Ismaa'aeel,* ◊ **And mention in the Book, Ismaa'aeel. Verily, he was true to what he promised, and he was a Messenger, and a Prophet. And he used to enjoin on his family and his people the ritual prayers and the obligatory charity, and his Lord was pleased with him.** ◊ *-(Surah Maryam: 54-55)*

*As such, it is only proper that we model ourselves after the prophets and the best of people, and be concerned with the state of the members of our households. Do not be neglectful of them, oh*

*worshipper of Allaah! Regardless of whether it is concerning your wife, your mother, father, grandfather, grandmother, your brothers, or your children; it is upon you to strive diligently in correcting their state and condition..."*
*(Collection of Various Rulings and Statements- Sheikh 'Abdul-'Azeez Ibn 'Abdullah Ibn Baaz, Vol. 6, page 47)*

CONTENT & STRUCTURE:

We hope to contribute works which enable every striving Muslim who acknowledges the proper position of the scholars, to fulfill the recognized duty and obligation which lays upon each one of us to bring the light of Islaam into our own lives as individuals, as well as into our homes and among our families. Towards this goal we are committed to developing educational publications and comprehensive educational curricula -through cooperation with and based upon the works of the scholars of Islaam and the students of knowledge. Works which, with the assistance of Allaah, the Most High, we can utilize to educate and instruct ourselves, our families and our communities upon Islaam in both principle and practice. The publications and works of the Nakhlah Educational Series are divided into the following categories:

*Basic / Elementary: Ages 4-11*
*Secondary: Ages 11-14*
*High School: Ages 14- Young Adult*
*General: Young Adult –Adult*
*Supplementary: All Ages*

Publications and works within these stated levels will, with the permission of Allaah, encompass different beneficial areas and subjects, and will be offered in every permissible form of media and medium. Certainly, the guiding scholar Sheikh Saaleh ibn Fauzaan al-Fauzaan, may Allaah preserve him, has stated,

*"Beneficial knowledge is itself divided into two categories. Firstly is that knowledge which is tremendous in its benefit, as it benefits in this world and continues to benefit in the Hereafter. This is religious Sharee'ah knowledge. And second, that which is limited and restricted to matters related to the life of this world, such as learning the processes of manufacturing various goods. This is a category of knowledge related specifically to worldly affairs.*
*...As for the learning of worldly knowledge, such as knowledge of manufacturing, then it is legislated upon us collectively to learn whatever the Muslims have a need for. Yet, if they do not have a need for this knowledge, then learning it is a neutral matter upon the condition that it does not compete with or displace any areas of Sharee'ah knowledge..."*
*("Explanations of the Mistakes of Some Writers", Pages 10-12)*
So we strive always to remind ourselves and our brothers of this crucial point also indicated by Sheikh Sadeeq Ibn Hasan al-Qanoojee, may Allaah have mercy upon him, in: *'Abjad al-'Uloom'*, (page 89)
*"...What is intended by knowledge in the mentioned hadeeth is knowledge of the religion and the distinctive Sharee'ah, knowledge of the Noble Book and the pure Sunnah, of which there is no third along with them. But what is not meant in this narration are those invented areas of knowledge,*

MISSION

*whether they emerged in previous ages or today's world, which the people in these present times have devoted themselves to. They have specifically dedicated themselves to them in a manner which prevents them from looking towards those areas of knowledge related to faith, and in a way which has preoccupied them from occupying themselves from what is actually wanted or desired by Allaah, the Most High, and His Messenger, who is the leader of men and Jinn. Due to this, the knowledge in the Qur'aan has become something abandoned and the sciences of hadeeth have become obscure, while these new areas of knowledge related to manufacturing and production continually emerge from the nations of disbelief and apostasy, and they are called, "sciences", "arts", and "ideal development". This sad state increases every day, indeed from Allaah we came and to Him shall we return....*

*...Additionally, although the various areas of beneficial knowledge all share some level of value, they all have differing importance and ranks. Among them is that which is to be considered according to its subject, such as medicine, and its subject is the human body. Or such as the sciences of 'tafseer' and its subject is the explanation of the words of Allaah, the Most Exalted and Most High, and the value of these two areas is not in any way unrecognized.*

*And from among the various areas, there are those areas which are considered according to their objective, such as knowledge of upright character, and its goal is understanding the beneficial merits that an individual can come to possess. And from among them there are those areas which are considered according to the people's need for them, such as 'fiqh' which the need for it is urgent and essential. And from among them there are those areas which are considered according to their apparent strength, such as knowledge of physical sports and exercise, as it is something openly demonstrated.*

*And from the areas of knowledge are those areas which rise in their position of importance through their combining all these different matters within them, or the majority of them, such as revealed religious knowledge, as its subject is indeed esteemed, its objective one of true merit, and its need is undeniably felt. Likewise one area of knowledge may be considered of superior rank than another in consideration of the results that it brings forth, or the strength of its outward manifestation, or due to the essentialness of its objective. Similarly, the result that an area produces is certainly of higher estimation and significance in appraisal than the outward or apparent significance of some other areas of knowledge.*

*For that reason, the highest ranking and most valuable area of knowledge is that of knowledge of Allaah the Most Perfect and the Most High, of His angels, and messengers, and all the particulars of these beliefs, as its result is that of eternal and continuing happiness."*

We ask Allaah, the most High to bless us with success in contributing to the many efforts of our Muslim brothers and sisters committed to raising themselves as individuals, and the next generation of our children, upon that Islaam which Allaah has perfected and chosen for us, and which He has enabled the guided Muslims to proceed upon in each and every century. We ask him to forgive us, and forgive the Muslim men and the Muslim women, and to guide all the believers to everything He loves and is pleased with. The success is from Allaah, the Most High the Most Exalted, alone and all praise is due to Him.

*Abu Sukhailah Khalil Ibn-Abelahyi*
*Taalib al-Ilm Educational Resources*

# Taalib al-Ilm Educational Publications is looking for

## Distributors:

We are working to make Taalib al-Ilm Education Resources publications available through distributors worldwide. Our present discounts for wholesalers are:

**50%** discount for any order of **USD $1000** or over retail cost

**60%** discount for any order of **USD $2000** or over retail cost

For further information, please contact the sales department by e-mail: *service@taalib.com.*

## Publication Contributors:

Additionally, in an effort to further expand our publication library, we are seeking contributing authors, translators, and compilers with beneficial works of any area of Sharee'ah knowledge for submission of their works for potential publication by us. For details and all submission guidelines please email us at: *service@taalib.com*

**Referral bonus:** *Individuals who refer a new distributor or publication contributor to us can receive a **$25 PayPal payment** upon:*

*1) a confirmed contract with a publication contributor or*

*2) receipt of a newly referred distributor's initial order at the 50% discount level.*

*Contact us for further information and conditions.*

MISSION

BELIEFS & WORSHIP

# 30 Days of Guidance [Book 1]:
## Learning Fundamental Principles of Islaam

*A Short Journey Within the Work al-Ibaanah al-Sughrah With*

# Sheikh 'Abdul-Azeez Ibn 'Abdullah ar-Raajhee
### (may Allaah preserve him)

*The Importance Of Asking To Be Guided In What You Say & Do * The Clear Guidance Of The Final Messenger Is For All Humanity * There Is A Single Straight Path Surrounded By Other False Paths * Every Ummah Divided But Those Upon The Truth Remain * Allaah Is With Those Who Remained Upon Revealed Guidance * Allaah Has Ordered Us To Stand United Upon The Truth & Not Divide * Every Name That Opposes The Guidance Of The Sunnah Is Rejected * The Strangeness Of Islaam Is Something Expected * That One Individual Whose Religion You Should Stand Upon * The Sunnah Is Revealed Knowledge From Allaah * Hold Firmly To The Sunnah As The Rope Of Allaah * Success Is To The Degree You Adhere To The Sunnah * The Incredible Reward For Firmly Holding To The Sunnah * Follow The Prophet's Sunnah & That Of His Guided Successors * Do Not Speak Against The Best Of Generations * Know That Knowledge Is Received And Can Be Lost * The Reality of the People of Misguidance & Their Deceptions * The Believers Are Distinct Upon Revealed Guidance * Advice of The Companions 'Uthman, 'Alee & Ibn 'Abbaas * Those Astray Turned Away From The Guidance Brought To Them * The People Of Misguidance Want You To Turn From Revealed Guidance * Those Who Debate Frequently Change Their Religion * The Blessing of Learning the Sunnah When Young * The Importance Of Both Loving & Hating For Allaah's Sake * A Person Stands Upon The Religion Of His Close Companion * Innovation That Is Disbelief Destroys All Ones' Good Deeds * Innovations In Islaam May Mislead You To Leave Islaam * The One Who Changes Islaam Is Cursed By Allaah & Creation * Repentance from Innovation Must Be Clear & Apparent * What Religion Will You Die Upon?*

*Compiled and Translated by:*
Abu Sukhailah Khalil Ibn-Abelahyi

[Available: **Now** ¦ price: **(SS) $27.50  (DS) $25**
**(W) $12** ¦ **(Kindle) $9.99**]

*An Educational Course Based Upon:*

# Beneficial Answers to Questions On Innovated Methodologies

*By the Guiding Scholar*

## Sheikh Saaleh Ibn Fauzaan al-Fauzaan

### (may Allaah preserve him)

This course focuses upon the importance of clarity in the way you understand and practice Islaam, in the midst of today's confusing claims to Islaam.

What is the right way, or methodology, to practice Islaam? Examine evidences and proofs from the source texts of the Qur'aan and Sunnah, along with the statements of many scholars explaining them, which connect you directly to that Islaam which the Messenger of Allaah ﷺ taught his Companions, may Allaah be pleased with them all.

## *Course Features:*

Twenty concise illustrated lessons to facilitate learning & review, with several important textual & course appendices.

*Compiled and Translated by:*

Abu Sukhailah Khalil Ibn-Abelahyi

[Available: **Now** ¦ price: **(SS) $30  (DS) $27.50 (W) $12** ¦ **(Kindle) $9.99**]

PREVIEW

*Lessons & Benefits From the Two Excellent Works:*

# The Belief of Every Muslim & The Methodology of The Saved Sect

### By the Guiding Scholar

## Sheikh Muhammad Ibn Jameel Zaynoo

### (may Allaah preserve him)

*This course begins with three full lessons with specific practical guidelines on how to effectively study Islaam and gain the knowledge needed to build your life as a Muslim into a life which is pleasing to Allaah.*

*Through twenty lessons on knowledge, beliefs, & methodology along with quizzes, review questions & lesson benefits -the remaining lessons take simply explained passages from two beneficial works that cover many important principles and the common misconceptions connected to them, which are fundamental to correctly understanding Islaam as it was taught to the Companions of the Messenger of Allaah.*

*Compiled and Translated by:*

Abu Sukhailah Khalil Ibn-Abelahyi

[Available: **Now** ¦ price: **(SS) $27.50  (DS) $25 (W) $12** ¦ **(Kindle) $9.99**]

PREVIEW

# Statements of the Guiding Scholars of Our Age
## *Regarding Books & their Advice to the Beginner Seeker of Knowledge*

*with Selections from the Following Scholars:*

*Sheikh 'Abdul-'Azeez ibn 'Abdullah ibn Baaz -Sheikh Muhammad ibn Saaleh al-'Utheimein - Sheikh Muhammad Naasiruddeen al-Albaanee - Sheikh Muqbil ibn Haadee al-Waada'ee - Sheikh 'Abdur-Rahman ibn Naaser as-Sa'adee - Sheikh Muhammad 'Amaan al-Jaamee - Sheikh Muhammad al-Ameen ash-Shanqeetee - Sheikh Ahmad ibn Yahya an-Najmee*
*(May Allaah have mercy upon them)*

*Sheikh Saaleh Fauzaan ibn 'Abdullah al-Fauzaan - Sheikh Saaleh ibn 'Abdul-'Azeez Aal-Sheikh - Sheikh Muhammad ibn 'Abdul-Wahhab al-Wasaabee -Permanent Committee to Scholastic Research & Issuing Of Islamic Rulings*
*(May Allaah preserve them.)*

### *Book Sections:*

*1. Guidance and Direction for Every Male and Female Muslim*

*2. Golden Advice that Benefits the Beginner Regarding Acquiring Knowledge*

*3. Beneficial Guidance for Female Students of Sharee'ah Knowledge*

*4 Guidance from the Scholars Regarding Important Books to Acquire for Seeking Knowledge*

*5. The Warning of the Scholars from the Books of those who have Deviated &*
*the Means and Ways of Going Astray*

*6. Clear Statements from the Scholars' Advice Regarding Memorizing Knowledge*

*7. Issues Related to the Verifiers of Books in our Age*

*Compiled and Translated by:*

Abu Sukhailah Khalil Ibn-Abelahyi

[Available: **Now** ¦ price: **(HB) $32.50  (SB) $25**
¦ **(Kindle) $9.99**]

PREVIEW

# A Lighthouse of Knowledge
## From A Guardian of the Sunnah [Books 1 & 2]

## Sheikh 'Rabee'a Ibn Haadee 'Umair al-Madkhalee
(may Allaah preserve him)

**Book 1: Unity, Advice, Brotherhood & the Call to Allaah {Section 1 - 5]**
**Book 2: The Connection with the People of Knowledge, Affairs of Brotherhood & Other Benefits [Section 1 - 8]**

*Appendices from the statements of some of the well known major scholars of this age*

***Appendix 1:*** Clarification From Sheikh Muqbil Ibn Haadee Al-Waadi'ee, May Allaah Have Mercy Upon Him, Regarding The Positions of Two Groups of People In Regard to Warning and Refutations

***Appendix 2:*** Clarification From Sheikh Muhammad Naasiruddeen Al-Albaanee, May Allaah Have Mercy Upon Him, Regarding The Role And Place Of Harshness

***Appendix 3:*** Clarification From Sheikh Saaleh al-Fauzaan Regarding The Final Position Of Sheikh Abdul-'Azeez Ibn Baaz, May Allaah Have Mercy Upon Him, Towards The Group Jama'at At-Tableegh

***Appendix 4:*** Clarification From Sheikh Ahmad An-Najmee, May Allaah Have Mercy Upon Him, That Advising The Muslims Through Refutations Is From The Way Of The First Generations Of Muslims

***Appendix 5:*** Clarification From Sheikh Saaleh al-Fauzaan Regarding The Falsehood of Those Who State That We Should Not Declare the One Who Opposes the Truth as Mistaken Or Wrong

***Appendix 6:*** Clarification From Sheikh Muhammad Ibn Saaleh al-'Utheimeen, May Allaah Have Mercy Upon Him, Regarding Various Concepts and Principles That Conflict With the Way of the Salaf

***Appendix 7:*** Clarification From Sheikh Muqbil Ibn Haadee Al-Waadi'ee, May Allaah Have Mercy Upon Him, Regarding The Matters Obligatory Upon The Muslims in Order to Achieve Unity

***Appendix 8:*** Clarification From Sheikh 'Abdul-'Azeez Ibn 'Abdullah Ibn Baaz, May Allaah Have Mercy Upon Him, Regarding the Responsibility of the Student of Knowledge to Himself and His Society

*Compiled and Translated by:* Abu Sukhailah Khalil Ibn-Abelahyi

[Available: **Now** ¦ price: **(SB) $25 (HB) $30** ¦ **(Kindle) $9.99**]

METHODOLOGY & SECTS

# The Cure, The Explanation, The Clear Affair, & The Brilliantly Distinct Signpost [Part 1]

*A Step by Step Educational Course on Islaam
Based upon Commentaries of*

## 'Usul as-Sunnah' of Imaam Ahmad
(may Allaah have mercy upon him)

This initial course book, which is part of a full series, can be vital learning tool, by Allah's persmission, for discussing and learning many of the most important beliefs of Islaam, how to implement them, and how to avoid common mistakes and misunderstandings. This full course series is based upon various commentaries of the original text, from the following scholars of our age, may Allaah preserve them all:

- Sheikh Zayd Ibn Muhammad al-Madkhalee
- Sheikh Saleeh Ibn Sa'd As-Suhaaymee
- Sheikh 'Abdul-'Azeez Ibn 'Abdullah ar-Raajhee
- Sheikh Rabee'a Ibn Haadee al-Madkhalee
- Sheikh Sa'd Ibn Naasir as-Shathree
- Sheikh 'Ubayd Ibn 'Abdullah al-Jaabiree
- Sheikh 'Abdullah Al-Bukharee
- Sheikh Hamaad Uthmaan
-

Each course book lesson has: lesson text, scholastic commentary, evidence summary, lesson benefits, standard & review exercises, as well as the Arabic text & translation of 'Usul as-Sunnah' in Arabic divided for easier memorization.

*Compiled and Translated by:*

Abu Sukhailah Khalil Ibn-Abelahyi

[Available: **TBA**¦ price: **(SS) $27.50 (DS) $25 (W) $12** ¦ **(Kindle) $9.99**]

PREVIEW

VARIOUS SUBJECTS

# *Whispers of Paradise (1):*

# *A Muslim Woman's Life Journal*

## An Islamic Daily Journal Which Encourages Reflection & Rectification

*Abu Alee ath-Thaqafee said: Abu Hafs used to say:*
*"The one who does not each moment weigh his situation*
*and condition against the scale of the Book of Allaah and*
*the Sunnah, and does not question his very footsteps,*
*then he is not to be considered worthy."*
(Seyaar 'Alaam an-Nubala: vol. 12, page 512)

*12 Monthly calendar pages* with beneficial quotations
from Ibn Qayyim & *Daily journal page* based upon
Hijree calendar(with corresponding C.E. dates)

## Each daily journal page starts with one of the following:

-*A Verse from the Noble Qur'aan*

-*An Authentic Narration of the Messenger of Allaah*

-*An Authentic Supplication*

-*A Beneficial Point from a Biography of the*
*Early Generations*

-*A Beneficial Statement from One of the*
*Well Known Scholars, Past or Present*

Available: **Now** ¦ price: **$25**
*[New elegantly designed edition for each year]*